With Compliments of the Author.

THE BEST MODE

OF

WORKING A PARISH

CONSIDERED IN

A Course of Lectures

DELIVERED IN DENVER CATHEDRAL, JANUARY
AND FEBRUARY, 1888,

AND IN SOME

Sermons

PREPARED FOR VARIOUS OCCASIONS.

BY

JOHN F. SPALDING, S. T. D.,

Bishop of Colorado.

AUTHOR OF "A MANUAL FOR MOTHERS' MEETINGS," "THE CHURCH
AND ITS APOSTOLIC MINISTRY," ETC.

MILWAUKEE, WIS.:
THE YOUNG CHURCHMAN CO.
1888.

18555

KING, FOWLE & CO., PRINTERS,
MILWAUKEE.

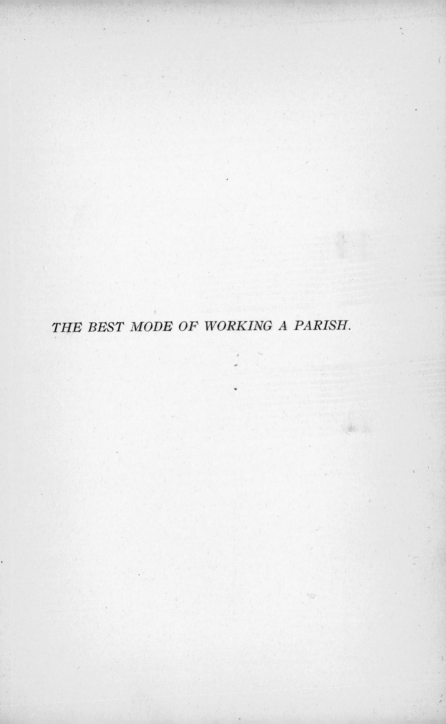

THE BEST MODE OF WORKING A PARISH.

- BY THE SAME AUTHOR :

THE CHURCH AND ITS APOS-
TOLIC MINISTRY.

A Course of Lectures delivered in
St. Mark's Church, Denver, in January, 1887. 12mo, 185 pp. Price, $1.00,
net.

———

THE THREE-FOLD MINISTRY
OF THE
CHURCH OF CHRIST.

A pamphlet. Price, 10 cents.

PUBLISHED BY
THE YOUNG CHURCHMAN COMPANY.

CONTENTS.

PART I.

THE BEST MODE OF WORKING A PARISH.

PART II.

PRINCIPLES OF CHURCH LIFE AND WORK.

TO

THE CLERGY AND LAITY

OF THE DIOCESE OF COLORADO

This Volume is Affectionately Dedicated,

WITH THE PRAYER AND IN THE HOPE

that it may be generally circulated and carefully read; that
large portions of it may be profitably used in lay reading;
and that the principles it inculcates may be duly
enforced in preaching, to the intent that all
the members of the Church may become intelligent and earnest workers for Christ, and that
through their efforts

THE GOSPEL OF THE KINGDOM MAY THE BETTER
FULFIL ITS GREAT MISSION

towards the masses of the people, for whose
temporal and spiritual welfare it is
the only effectual agency.

I.

INTRODUCTION.

S. Matt. x, 42 : And whosoever shall give to drink unto one of these little ones a cup of cold water only in the name of a disciple, verily I say unto you, he shall in no wise lose his reward.

WE infer from these words a general principle. It follows that every Christian has a ministry on behalf of others, and that his reward is conditioned on his faithfulness in fulfilling it. A cup of cold water given to the thirsty is the least service one could do for another. By every Christian Disciple it would be given as freely to the least of Christ's suffering poor as to his own equals or superiors. But even so slight a service as this, done from love to Christ, cannot be unrewarded. Leaving out of view the final awards of the day of recompense, it has *its own* reward, which is not contingent, nor possible of failure : it is the consciousness of well doing—the sweetest of all enjoyments. Service of Christ is sacrifice for others. Reward is proportioned to the degree of service. If the

9

least service is thus rewarded, surely all service must be. There can be no service done to others in the name of Christ that shall fail of its attendant blessing.

We are not to suppose it left to our option to give the cup of cold water and all else it symbolizes, or not. We must do it, as we are Christians. Not only is it enjoined; it is essential to our Christian character. There must be in us such a disposition as will impel us to do it; otherwise it is not Christian service and there is no reward. Failing herein, we are not living Christians. We stand on a like footing with unbelievers in Christ, if we do not possess and exemplify a spirit of active Christian beneficence.

I do not now speak of the reward. It is right, indeed, to have it in view. Hope is a natural principle of action. Many a good man has been animated to a life of strenuous endeavor or to patience under intense suffering, by the anticipation of the benefits accruing, and the crown that is the reward of fidelity. But it is not merely the hope of reward that actuates the Christian. The same character and conduct would be required, though nothing were to be gained by it. The life should be determined by the constraining love of Christ. We should do good because it is commanded. But our obedience to divine commands should be our highest pleasure. The disposition, the bent of the mind and heart should be such, that it will be our very meat and drink to do the will of God. Christianity is not what has been sneeringly called "other worldliness." The truest Christian is one who habitually forgets self in the earnestness of his work for Christ and his fellow-men. He best works out his own salvation whose end is Christian service. He that would save his life must lose it. He who loses his own life in the vocation and ministry of the Christian, the same shall find it. (S. Matt. x, 39.)

The Christian is one who is regenerate; that is to say, one in whom Christ is born. Being in Christ, it follows that Christ is in him, the animating principle of his true being, for regeneration is not only the being born into Christ's Kingdom, its environment of privileges and means of grace. It not only puts you in the state of salvation and under the responsibilities of a heavenly citizenship. It is the reception through Christ's Spirit of Christ's own life. It ensures membership of His Body. It grafts you into the corporate life of His Divine Humanity, in which you live as He liveth in you. It gives you in the Church the essential life of Him Who said, "I am the way, the truth and the life," " Whoso eateth My flesh and drinketh My blood hath eternal life," and "because I live, ye shall live also." They who are regenerate should let this Life within them mould their whole character and determine their conduct and conversation. They should simply act out the life of Christ that is in them, and thus live in their regenerate being, not in that which is of the old nature. Thus they should prove that they are new creatures. (Gal. vi, 15; 2 Cor. v, 17.)

Every kind of life must have its manifestations. Life in the organism must show itself, else there is torpor, the actuality, or at least the semblance of death. Occasionally you may see a tree or a plant of which it is impossible to tell from its exterior appearance whether it be alive or dead. This is the spiritual condition of many professing Christians. But ordinarily life induces growth and the manifestations, the activities suitable to its nature. There is the budding, the leafage, the flower and the fruit. Everybody knows how the carnal, worldly life of men manifests and proves itself. What exertions it leads to, what energy, what zeal, what perseverance, what sacrifices of time and ease! What dangers it encounters to compass its ends, to acquire the means of ministering to its pleasures, to gain the wealth to satisfy its greeds, to win the place or power coveted by its ambition. Such is life in and of the world. Why should it not be so of spiritual life, life in Christ? How can it be hidden, inert and torpid? How can it be that he who has it in him does not act according to its promptings? Is the Christ life in us? The outward conduct must show it. We must live out the life within. Hear S. Paul teaching us: "The life that I now live in the flesh, I live by the faith of the Son of God, Who died for me and rose again," and "Christ liveth in me."

Now, what will be the outward life of one thus regenerate and thereupon spiritually renewed? What are the natural manifestations of the life of Christ in those who let it actuate and determine them, and freely show it in conduct? We can learn the answer by study of the life of Christ. What He did, that should we do. His aim, purpose, all-controlling motive should be ours. His life being in us, we must in all things be like Him. He came to do the will of Him that sent Him, and to finish His work. He loved God supremely. His constant worship and service of God His Father, was the perfect expression of His love. He gave His whole strength to God's service. It was an obedience even unto death. He took up His cross and bore it steadily, even in mortal suffering and agony. In eternity His purposes were, "Lo, I come to do Thy will, O God; I am content to do it: yea, Thy law is within My heart;" and through all and for our sakes, in the pursuance of His work, He perfected Himself, resisting the Tempter and overcoming temptation, and thus obtained for us new strength and the ministry of angels, and through His death unto sin, the life of the resurrection It is ours, in like manner, in Him to love, and worship, and serve God; to obey Him, regardless of consequences; to bear our daily cross of self-denial and sacrifice; to die with Him unto sin; to rise with Him, to enter into His victory and His joy.

But if there is anything that peculiarly strikes us in the life of Christ when on earth, it is His Ministry on be-

half of others. His service of God was for the salvation
of men. He came down from heaven, leaving all its glo-
ries which He had with the Father, as the Creed states it,
"for us men and for our salvation." He took upon Him
our humiliation for a great Ministry on behalf of the sinful and the suffering. He came, bringing Redemption
from sin and all its consequent evils and miseries. He
lived here only to bestow it, to bring men to receive it,
to remove the infirmities, pains and sorrows, of which it
is the only antidote. Thus He offered freely to all, pardon, healing, life, and an immortality of blessedness.
Thus He lifted up the slaves of sin from their bondage,
broke their fetters, took them by the hand and bade them
rise to a new life of purity, and freedom, and love, and
duty. Thus He wrought His miracles of mercy, healing
the sick, restoring the maimed, giving sight to the blind,
and to the infirm and decrepit the vigor and joy of health.
His benefits were not partial. There was no want of man
which He was not ready to supply, no disease to which He
did not apply the remedy, no suffering which He did not
alleviate, no sorrow which He did not console. In every
sense, temporal and spiritual, whether of the Body or of
the Soul, He was man's Redeemer. With what fulness of
meaning it was said of Him, that "He went about doing
good."

We must participate in His work. The motive, the
aim, the purpose, are essential. Entered, as we are, into

His life, we must live it. We must do the works which
He did. We may not, indeed, wield for the good of men
the powers of nature, using her laws, controlling her
operations; but with the right motive, the right disposition of heart, and the right endeavor, we can do works
bearing at least some real likeness to His. If we do but
let the life that is in us as Christians, determine our purposes and efforts, we can bestow some measure of temporal
and spiritual blessing upon the needy, the suffering and
the sinful. If we cannot confer pardon, we can bring the
sinner to Christ. If we cannot heal with a word, nor
remove at our option the diseases which manifest the
effects of sin, we can command the natural methods. We
can care for the sick. We can bind up the wounds of the
stricken, bleeding and broken-hearted. We can give
whatever relief our personal attendance can administer,
or our influence or our means can procure. We can, as
our Lord did, bear the griefs, and infirmities, and sicknesses of men upon our sympathy. We can suffer with
and for them. So we can console the wretched, and give
to the poor and suffering our active, helpful compassion,
and our effectual fervent prayers. Having Christ in us,
why should we not, in some feeble way it may be, and far
behind Him, but still truly follow Him and represent
Him, and do the works which He left for us, for His
Body, the Church, to accomplish—the like works in our
day for those among whom He has placed us, to those

which He did as He went about among the sorrowing and
the sinful, in Judæa, Samaria and Galilee? Why can we
not, why should we not, with Him, His life by His Spirit
energizing us, go about doing good?

By His Life, and Death, and Resurrection, He has
accomplished, for all, Redemption. All whose nature He
assumed, and for whom He lived, and died, and rose, and
ascended, are redeemed. But they do not know it. It is
to be made known to them. They are to be prepared for
its reception. It is to be proclaimed everywhere. It is to
be conferred and made effective upon all. To this end is
the Church. To this end we are in Christ. They who
have received it are to impart it. The Church, Christ's
Body, is here, to carry on and to complete the work which
Christ Himself began to do and to teach in His ministry
on earth (Acts i, 1); the Church, by her ministry, and by
all her members, by all her gifts and instrumentalities.
Whatever her forces, she must bring them into effective
operation.

What are we doing, brethren, to carry on Christ's
work? Where are the sin-sick souls whom we have
brought to Christ for His healing? Where are the poor
to whom, through our efforts, the Blessed Gospel is
preached? Where are the sorrowing to whom we have
brought consolation? Where are the mourners whom we
have comforted, the hungry we have fed, the sick we have
visited? Where are the wretched whose infirmities we

have borne? Where are those to whom we have given the cup of cold water in the name of Christ, with all the good things, temporal and spiritual, which this signifies? Where are the proofs that we are Christians? Doubtless some of you would bear the tests. But must we not all, conscious of our failures to be and to do what our Lord requires of us, resolve anew to be henceforth more faithful to our vocation and ministry, especially when we seek, as we are invited this morning to do, in the Holy Communion, that all-sufficient grace and strength that comes from spiritually eating and drinking the Flesh and Blood of Christ?

II.

Daniel xi, 33: They that understand among the people shall instruct many.

TRUE religion is never the result of intuitive knowledge. It must always be imparted. It comes from definite instruction. Left to themselves and the light of nature, men gain religious ideas of the most variant and contradictory character, and of questionable moral influence. No religion except Christianity has ever made morals or virtue its chief aim. Religion and morality, as judged by all other religions, have had no necessary connection. If some systems of Christianity have yielded to this practical divorce of religion from goodness of character, as may be seen in the historical developments of religious error, it is clear that we must accept the Christian religion as it is divinely given, as its Founder taught it and exemplified it in His Divine Human Life on earth, and as always held by "the Church of the Living God, the pillar and ground of the Truth."

Our religion is objective, and hence it must be learned. It cannot be self-evolved from our own minds. The

18

brightest and best of men, rejecting external aids and endeavoring to think out and frame a religious system of their own from the elements of religious thought that have somehow come to be entertained, are certain to be led astray by false lights, and to grope their life-long way in darkness and delusion. The human mind is adapted to receive the truths of Christianity, and naturally craves, but is unable of itself to discover them. Such is the teaching of all history and all experience.

God is the author and source of all true religious knowledge. Granted that we can arrive naturally at some faint, inadequate idea of Him, all right apprehension of His nature and attributes has actually come to us, as of necessity it must come, from Revelation. The works of God but imperfectly reveal Him. The written Word is of prime importance. They who would impart religious knowledge must receive it from its source. All true religion is revealed, hence the authority it possesses. It is given to man because he needs it and is not complete without it. It must be taught him and learned by him, to enable him to fulfill the purposes of his being and to enter into the sphere of spiritual life, in which is the perfection of his nature.

Christianity is the full, completed Revelation. The Church is its embodiment. The Church witnesses to, preserves and hands it on and proclaims it. The Church is to make known in the Christian scheme the manifold wisdom of God. (Eph. iii, 10.) Teaching is the great function of the Church. The office of the Christian teacher assumes the highest importance. He is to make known to all men the religion which is revealed of God in Christ, by which alone it is possible to live rightly or to die happily.

The preaching of the Word, or the giving of religious instruction, is one of the principal duties of the Christian Ministry, but it does not belong to them exclusively. If the Church had not her fixed, unvarying Faith, defined authoritatively, and received of all her children, it might have been necessary to restrict religious teaching to the specially authorized "Ministers of Christ and Stewards of the Mysteries of God." But such restriction has never prevailed in the Church. Whenever her life has been most effectively exhibited, she has used her laity as helpers to the Ministry in teaching, and in her various branches of practical work. "The brethren" were teachers according to their ability in Apostolic times, as the "Acts of the Apostles" witnesses. In the primitive Church there were distinguished lay preachers, apologists and teachers. In the catechetical instruction of the young and the immature of mind, as well as in the various works of Christian charity, the Clergy have always had the assistance of the laity, both men and women. And how invaluable has been the help in religious teaching of qualified laymen upon themes both of doctrine and duty, is illustrated in modern as well as in ancient times by many notable examples.

Nor does it need such precedents to show that they who understand among the people must instruct others. " Ye are an holy Priesthood," says S. Peter in a catholic or general Epistle. The Priest's lips must not only keep knowledge, but impart it. It was to be a characteristic of the dispensation of the Spirit that all the people called of God should prophesy (Joel ii, 28; Acts ii, 17). All who have received the Word and Spirit of Christ must speak for God and tell what the Lord hath done for their souls. If the salvation of the soul and the whole future destiny in this life and in eternity depends on obedience to the will of God, every one who believes this and who accepts Christianity as the revelation of God's will, and feels its value and blessedness, must commend it by word and act. The Christian who appreciates the Faith of Christ will be unable to refrain from making it known. He must act upon the golden rule of right and duty and labor to confer upon others the blessings he enjoys.

How is this work to be done? How can you, who have been to some extent instructed, promote the religious instruction of others, of whatever class and whatever stage of intellectual development?

It is well to think first of the subjects of instruction, then of the means of conveying and adapting it so as to make it vital and effective to its ends.

Generally, it is evident that they who are to be taught Christianity are all mankind, people of all races. Christ died for all. The mission of the Church is to all. The power of Christ's Gospel has been abundantly shown in the elevation of the most degraded to the appreciation of its privileges and the enjoyment of its blessing. The fact has been made sufficiently clear that Christianity is adapted to the regeneration of all men, by the signal examples of its influence in raising to the highest type of character, men of what are called inferior and degraded races. We have among us the Chinese, the Negro, the Indian. Some of one or more of these are in most of our communities. We do not need to go to Africa or China to find them. We can begin our so-called foreign missionary work at home. There may be little romance in gathering in classes of these for Christian instruction. It is easier to take credit for missionary work that is done by proxy in far distant lands. But that the heathen are among us is a providential indication of our duty. These, as we ourselves are Christians, we must teach the saving knowledge of Jesus Christ.

But it is not those of foreign race that we now have specially in view. There is a vast mass of ignorance all about us in those kindred to us in blood and language. Judged by the highest standard of Christian knowledge, all are in ignorance, and all need enlightenment. Ignorance is relative. All have something to learn. All Christians have something to teach. The least in the Kingdom of God is in respect of knowledge greater than John the

Baptist, the last and greatest of the prophets before Christ; and greater by consequence than any who are still out of the Kingdom, and ignorant of the faith and of the elements of Christian duty. The learned of this world have often stood confounded by the wisdom of mere babes in Christ, because "the foolishness of God is wiser than men, and the weakness of God is stronger than men." There is no Christian who is not called to be a teacher in respect to those things which he knows, and a learner in respect to those things of which he is ignorant. All who are out of Christ are to be led to Him and assisted to the attainment of a right faith and the spirit of love and obedience, by all those who have the truth and know the way. I need not qualify this by saying all who have opportunities, for opportunities are to be made. Watchfulness, interest and earnest effort will easily find them.

Next to the unregenerate and unconverted are those whose faith is imperfect, those whose impressions or ideas of Christianity have come from their associations in a society that is nominally Christian, or who are the passive adherents of one or other of the variant sectarian systems in which there is always a combination of partial truth and partial error. It is usually dangerous to attack and destroy what faith a man has, even though it be defective; but it is always right, and always a duty, to seek to supplement it, and give it accuracy and completeness. Hence, all who are under the influence of the imperfect or erroneous systems referred to, the unconscious victims of any of the "isms," which are the reproach of Christianity and the main obstacles to that unity of faith and order for which the Lord prayed (S. John, xvii), and His Apostles labored (1 Cor., iii), are to be led back to the primitive, Apostolic and catholic position, the true resting-place and ark of safety for saints and sinners.

But we are to have in view, especially, what are called the masses, the laboring men, who are the most numerous, and most important class in every community, and who are, to a large extent, alienated from Christianity. They are in danger now of coming under organized influences which are hostile to the Church. Secularism, Socialism, Anarchism, are claiming the allegiance of working men, and by specious sophistries arraying them against the faith that alone can really befriend them, and bestow what they really want. For it is Christianity alone that, by the Incarnation of the Son of God, levels all caste and race distinctions, and teaches practically that all men are brethren, and all "members one of another." These are to be conciliated and instructed, and shown their true interests. It is to be proved to them by deeds, how thoroughly and consistently Christianity recognizes the value of man as man, and how potent its instrumentalities to fulfill its great aim and purpose to elevate him in the scale of being, and enable him to attain his true place, and the dignity and glory of his manhood.

Finally, there is a most important subdivision of this class, the children and youth of families in moderate circumstances in the ordinary walks of life. Multitudes of these are growing up without religious knowledge or training, without God and without hope. What they learn in the streets is mostly evil. What they learn at school adds but little to their moral and religious culture. They are mostly deprived by their circumstances of any teaching in regard to the highest matters that concern immortal beings. Their higher spiritual reason and conscience is for the most part undeveloped and untrained.

It is not so difficult to teach the young as it is those who have reached maturity. Their minds are more receptive. Their hearts are more easily reached. They learn more easily. They have less to unlearn. Their habits of thought, feeling and conduct are not so fixed. The twig can be bent. The growth of the sapling can be directed, but the tree becomes rigid and immovable.

Of course, it is not meant that religious instruction is to be restricted to any class or classes of youth, or of adults who are children so far as concerns religious teaching and discipline. All require it. The effort is to be made persistently and with all the zeal and devotion of which loving hearts are capable, by all among the people who have understanding, to instruct the many. What a work is here! How can it be undertaken, and how carried on with success?

I must first call your attention to an agency of great efficiency and value: the publication and generous distribution of Bibles and Prayer Books, and of religious books and tracts specially prepared for popular effect. The press has become a mighty engine both of good and evil, and I believe the good predominates. It is a means of diffusing every kind and variety of information, assisting thoughtful minds among all classes to form intelligent opinions upon every conceivable topic of human interest. It promotes the habit of general reading, excites inquiry, advances the general intelligence. We must grant, indeed, that its multitudinous issues; its books of every description, of which it would take more time than most could command, to keep up a knowledge even of the titles ; its periodical literature, annual, semi-annual, quarterly, monthly, weekly and daily, which form the sole reading of most intelligent men, must inevitably tend to produce narrow, superficial, ill-formed minds and crude intellectual character. Still, the facilities it gives to the masses of the people of gaining information, the facts and truths it communicates, the thought it quickens, the intellectual culture it subserves, are more than a compensation. As an instance of its importance, which will be most readily appreciated : What an absurdity without it, would not universal suffrage become in a federated Republic like ours ? There are, indeed, multitudes who exercise this high prerogative of citizens without the slightest qualification. But how vastly greater would be the number, were not the facilities of gaining knowledge and forming accurate opinions so abundant. Every politician well knows the power of the press. It is wielded with success not only by the high-principled and patriotic, but also by the ambitious dema-gogue and the unscrupulous political charlatan. Its best uses have become indispensable to the safety of our insti-tutions. Its demoralization and abuse will too surely help on their destruction.

Surely, religion is justified in making large use of the press for its purposes of instruction. Sectaries of all de-scriptions have shown how effectually their tenets may be propagated through this agency. There is scarcely an intelligent person in the country who is not constantly receiving pamphlets and periodicals advocating the restoration of the Jewish Sabbath, giving information concerning the prophecies of the Lord's Second Advent, or the peculiar doctrines of Spiritualism or of Swedenbor-gianism. The extent and the volume of literature of these sorts is indeed surprising. It should teach us a lesson. It is the imperative duty of our Church people to sustain with like generosity our Bible and Prayer Book societies, and the publication of Church books, and tracts, and periodicals, and to be at least equally zealous in their cir-culation. By liberal support, by generous contributions, by all possible efforts to promote their wide distribution, we might vastly increase their usefulness.

There are few families in which there is no Bible, though it be dust-covered and seldom read. The Prayer Book is to us the best and indispensable companion to the Bible, for it is the authoritative guide in its interpretation, embodying all doctrine and teaching all duty, and turning both into prayer, thus securing the entrance into the heart of all truth, and building up the Spiritual life. Let every Churchman keep on hand a good supply of Prayer Books. Sell them to those who can purchase. Give them to those who cannot buy. Patiently and lovingly explain the services to those who will use them. It would be impossible to estimate the number of those whom the Prayer Book has led to the Saviour, and instructed in saving knowledge. In many a dwelling in the wilderness it has gone before the Church and has fulfilled the offices of both Church and Ministry, until these could be solicited and obtained. No other book but the Bible has guided and trained so many souls for heaven.

Next in value are popular books and tracts on practical religion and the doctrine, polity and usages of the Church. How many have been taught by Thomas à Kempis to imitate Christ; by Jeremy Taylor to live holily, and to die happily; by Bunyan to overcome their spiritual enemies in life's pilgrimage; by Keble to follow our Lord's life in the observances of the Christian year, and walk in His blessed footsteps. He who writes a good book, or a good hymn, is among the world's greatest benefactors. The precious treasures of Christian literature should be placed within reach of all. They who have understanding will spare no trouble or expense in this effort to instruct the people.

The great obstacle to the extension of the Church among the masses is ignorance and prejudice. Never was there a controversy with those who oppose us that did not greatly further our progress. Never was there a book or tract written with a high Christian motive and circulated and read in a dispassionate and prayerful spirit, that has not brought multitudes to rally beneath the standard of the Church. Chapman's " Sermons on the Church," Richardson's " Churchman's Reasons for His Faith and Practice," Kip's " Double Witness," Randall's "Why I Am a Churchman," Onderdonk's "Episcopacy Tested by Scripture," Timlow's "Plain Footprints," Little's "Reasons," and other like works should be in every Churchman's hands for generous and wide circulation among all people who would desire or can be induced to read them. Let us make full use of this agency, by which so much has been done and is doing, and make it as efficient as possible for Christ and the Church. Let us avail ourselves of the general fondness for reading. Let us give to the people a Christian literature, full of fact and of truth, and of divine and holy unction, such as will instruct, purify, reform and elevate the people. Infidelity is subsidizing the press to its own godless purposes. Every form of error and misbelief depends on the press for its advocacy. Let the truth have free course. Give it a fair field. Let it grapple with error and falsehood. The result can not be doubtful.

In this use of the press you must first become yourselves well instructed. Ignorance means indifference. With increasing knowledge there will be the growth of interest. Every family in the Church should take the best of the Church papers and periodicals. It is indispensable that you should be thoroughly conversant with the religious needs, with missionary intelligence at home and abroad, with all the various operations of the Church, Diocesan and General, and with the movements of thought and opinion in the Church and in the world about us. It is strange, indeed, that any intelligent Churchman should be content to remain in ignorance of the constitution of the Church ; its polity, history and doctrine, and usages ; its operations for human good; its progress; its wants; the instrumentalities employed in its extension. What is so indispensable to man individually and socially as Christianity ? What institution is of such priceless value as the Church? Better that the government we love should fail, than that the Church of God should fall into decay and barrenness. If you are citizens of Christ's Kingdom, you will be sure of a heavenly country, though the earthly should perish. Why not give your interest to the more important ? Why be indifferent to those things which are so intimately connected with the welfare of man here and forever? For your own good, as well as for the good you can do, you should acquire familiarity with all the facts and truths it behooves you to know in reference to Christianity and the Church of Christ. Then, knowing the truth, you must proclaim it. Have your Church books and pamphlets, and periodicals, as an armory from which to draw whatever arms and ammunition may be needed to repel assaults of unbelief and of sectarianism, and to fight the battles of the Church.

But you must remember that after all, invaluable as it may be made, the press can only be an ally. Bibles and tracts alone can never convert and reform the world. Much practical harm has come from the common delusion that to secure the salvation of the sinner, it is only necessary to put a Bible and a few good tracts into his hands. It will not do to put a book in place of the Ministry, and reading in the place of direct personal teaching. If it has been thought by some that the Bible and a few good books of devotion and practical religion, translated and generally circulated in heathen lands, would disperse and scatter the old heathen religions and superstitions like the mists before the rising sun, or that here at home Bible and tract distribution is the sure means of Christianizing the people, little experience is needed to show the fatal mistake. There are many who cannot read; there are more who will not; still more who would not understand if they did. In Apostolic and primitive times the Church made greatest

progress and wrought her most stupendous victories without books. Christianity had been orally taught throughout the world, and multitudes were thoroughly instructed
for the Kingdom of Heaven, partly before the New Testament had been written, and wholly before it had been collected in a volume and was in the hands of Christians.
The Apostolic method, long so successful, can never give
place to any other. The Church wants living teachers.
The book or tract will seldom, of itself, awaken interest.
This can ordinarily be done only by the living voice, from
the heart of love and sympathy. Most of those who are
indifferent to religion steel themselves against its influence.
There must be found in every man some impressible side,
some vulnerable point, at which your spiritual assaults
may be successful. There are none so hardened, none so
encased in unbelief and prejudice, that they may not be
softened and subdued, and won to Christ and the Church
by methods which a loving, gentle heart full of human
interest and sympathy, would find available. Gain the
attention, excite the interest, win the good-will and confidence; then give your book, point out what is to be read,
direct the manner of reading, and your time, expense and
effort will be at last rewarded. Times of trouble, affliction
or sickness, are precious opportunities not to be lost. The
heart is more tender and susceptible, if rightly approached.
In such times you may gain a ready ear for the truth, and

lead the weary and heavy-laden to the great source of rest and consolation.

But not confining your interest to these, let each member of the Church determine to make some person or persons the special object of prayer and intercession, leaving no effort untried to win their interest and lead them to Christ and His Church; can anybody doubt, that with God's help, success would in due time follow? How soon would you double your communicants and your stated worshippers. Even without that organized effort, by which the world has long since taught us the greatest results are attainable, each of you might bring in recruits for the Christian army from those of every age and rank in life. They would come gladly as volunteers, well instructed and eager for further knowledge. Each in turn would become a worker and a teacher. The many would be reached with the Gospel of love, and the truth of God's Word, which the Church upholds and proclaims, would be gloriously triumphant!

III.

Isa. xxviii, 9 : Whom shall he teach knowledge?
And whom shall he make to understand doctrine?
Them that are weaned from the milk and drawn
from the breasts.

ALL education begins in the family. Here first is the
field for Christian nurture. Here the Christian
knowledge, that is its chief instrument, is first imparted.
Here the holy influences so indispensable in promoting
it make their first and most indelible impressions. The baptized child is from the first the subject of grace. There is
no point assignable after baptism at which it is expected
to begin to grow "in the nurture and admonition of the
Lord." The Christian family is the original school of
Christ, "the Church that is in the house" (Col. iv, 15;
Rom. xvi, 5 ; 1 Cor. xvi, 19). Its training is continuous
from earliest youth to manhood. Its power is not les-
sened, whatever outward helps are afforded. The character is chiefly determined by the education that is im-
perceptibly received in the earliest years. Not more sure
in its results is heredity upon moral and intellectual
character in the offspring than is the influence of parental

34

training, through example, love, sympathy, associations, and positive instruction. This is the divine plan and order.

But in a certain stage of development the child perceives itself to be already a subject of other than family relations. It is a member of the State and of the Church. A training for the duties involved in these relations is necessary. The State must have its schools. The Church must institute her methods of instruction, her means for the moulding of character. These are the three divine institutions. In the family, in society, in the Church of Christ must all the education be afforded which is requisite for all life's duties and responsibilities. The subjects of one are to be the subjects of all. Each must be trained to filial obedience, to the rights and obligations of citizenship, to the functions and duties of immortal beings in the sphere of grace. Without the Church the education given, whether by the family or the State, alone, is inadequate. Christianity must permeate and mould the family, the State, the social organism, to make the training they can give effective for their own respective spheres. The Church must lend her aid in making good children and good citizens. Hence distinctively Christian education is necessary. It begins in the Christian family. It is to go on in the Christian school. It must be unintermitted in the wider school of life. The Church has in charge the nurture and discipline by which to attain the stature of true and complete manhood. To this end she is constituted the keeper and witness of the Word of Truth. She is to give to all the requisite instruction and insure to them the needed influences for their moral, intellectual and spiritual growth. She is to do all this by her Ministry of the Word, of prayer and Sacraments, by her pastoral care, by the examples of her Saints, by her environment of grace and holy associations, and not least by the direct personal influence and teaching of all her people.

The most important class of those who are to receive the care and instruction of the Church, are those whose minds are forming, the young in all stages of their progress, from the time they become cognizant of their Church relations. And we must include with these all whose minds are undeveloped and immature, who equally need religious instruction and training.

Thus we have the sufficient justification of the Sunday-school. It is an instrumentality employed by the Church in her teaching office. The Sunday-school is specially important, because the Church by its means, more than in any other way, calls out and utilizes the help of her laity.

We may admit that the Sunday-school is a modern device, an expedient. From the time Christianity gained ascendency in the world the Church largely controlled and directed all schools of learning, and education was more or less Christian. To learn the facts of the Christian Creed and the doctrines and moral principles of Chris-

tianity, was everywhere a part of education. Parish
Schools, Colleges, Universities, were Christian schools.
The training in these was supplemented by habitual catechizing by the Clergy. George Herbert's "Country Par-
son" represents the custom of his time, which had doubtless long prevailed, and continues in many parishes to the
present day. On Sunday afternoons a service was held
especially for youths and adults needing instruction.
Parents, employers and masters brought them to Church,
having first taught them at home. They joined in the
Common Prayer, and after the Second Lesson, the children and young people coming forward to the chancel,
were publicly examined and catechized. Leading questions would quicken attention and help to suggest the
answers. Thus the mind would be developed, the understanding instructed, and the heart improved. Many a
shaft of truth would strike home to the hearts of the
older members of the flock. All would become well
grounded in the elementary principles of Christian truth.
The Bible and Prayer Book, made the basis of teaching,
would become thoroughly familiar to the people. Thus
the foundations would be laid for a healthy, robust and
manly piety. So was it substantially in the early Church.
So, in her best days, has our Mother Church in England
trained her young and ignorant for the Christian life. It
is a great misfortune that this excellent method has been
suffered, to such an extent, to fall into disuse. Its revival

is, on all accounts, desirable. But even if revived and
brought into general use, the Sunday-school, in some
form, would still be necessary in these times.

Sunday-schools were originally for poor children and
others who had in an evil age—it was the latter part of
the 18th century—fallen outside the pale of the Church,
and were intellectually and spiritually uncared for. They
were called "ragged schools," because the children could
be gathered into them from the highways, from the miserable hovels of poverty, and from the slums of vice, in
the condition in which hearts of mercy sought them out
and found them, and instructed in the simple elements of
secular learning and in the Word of Life. Such they
were when first introduced into this country.

The Church won her first triumphs by " preaching the
Gospel to the poor." In the course of centuries, it came
at length to be preached chiefly to the rich, to those who
could pay for it, the poor having fallen beneath its influence and being thus excluded from its blessings. This is
the perversion of the Divine ordinance. The scope and
use of the Sunday-school have been similarly changed.
Within less than a century it was exclusively for those
who could not be instructed without it. Now it is too
commonly the children of well-to-do families of Christian
people, who can pay for seats in Church, to whom its
benefits are offered. For these the Sunday-school is made
to stand as sponsor, and to discharge the parents' duty

In some places it almost looks as if the Church stood aloof from her young, and was not expected to feed and nourish them, and extend to them her sheltering care until the time of their confirmation.

In some Christian bodies the Sunday-school seems fast becoming the only church of the children. It is losing all relations to the Church. Its features are more and more unchurchly. It seems to be adapted to unfit those who love it, to love and to be edified in the Church. Graduating at an early age from the Sunday-school, they are not prepared to take pleasure in the Church services, and hence they relapse into the world. Thus Sunday-schools may be of such a character as to be an evil. They may be a hindrance to the reception of the Gospel of Christ in the Church. Such they will certainly be, when they assume for children the place of the Church; when their promoters think and speak of them as the children's Church; when parents delegate to them their own duty of Christian teaching, and they abuse their trust, by making the Church, so far as the children are concerned, a nullity.

It is often said that the Sunday-school is the nursery of the Church. This conception, as often understood, involves the fatal error alluded to, though of course there is a sense in which it is true. The Sunday-school must not be made a *nursery* outside the Church, in which the young plants are to be trained to a certain degree of maturity, and then transplanted into the field of the Church. The Sunday-school must, to serve the ends which make it legitimate, be the very garden of the Lord. It must be a choice part of the field of her culture. It must be within, not without the Church. Its instrumentalities must be the Church's own. It must be thoroughly Churchly and Christian in all its methods. The Pastor must be, and be recognized as the head and chief instructor. The teachers must be Christians. The right use of the Prayer Book, training in worship, with heart and voice, is an essential part of its purpose. The early habit of public worship, devoutly and intelligently rendered, must be promoted. Then the Sunday-school may be of very great help and advantage.

We must take the Sunday-school as we find it, improve its excellencies and remedy its defects. Conservatism has long opposed it, except as restricted to its original purpose. There are many Churchmen who only speak of it in disparagement. They allege that it is needless ; that parents, and the Church by her ancient and proved methods of catechetical teaching, could do much more effectively what it is expected to do; that from the difficulty of getting competent teachers, they are forced to employ the young and inexperienced; that the teaching is often false and injurious; that the children swarm out into the streets at the time of service to desecrate the Lord's day: and so they go on through all the counts of the terrible indictment, which is, in the character of some Sunday-schools, for the most part justified.

But these objections do not apply in any such disastrous measure to the Sunday-schools of our own Church. We have the Sunday-school. It is a fact we must take account of. If we do not maintain, perfect and use it, the denominations which make much of it, will educate our children for us. We cannot rely on the other agencies which in former days were effective. We need not make it a substitute for any others. All approved means should be used. But we shall surely make a most fatal mistake, if we do not take the Sunday-school, which is so universally accepted and so generally popular, and make it what we feel it ought to be, and thoroughly use it as an agency which is our own—for it was in the Church that it had its origin—and make it, as we most unquestionably can, a blessed instrumentality of the Church.

Let us briefly consider some of the conditions of success. What are we to make of the Sunday-school? How are we to conduct it that it may be what it ought to be to us?

Whether the school is large or small, it should be graded into three departments : the infant school; the school for the young, till they are prepared for Confirmation, or later; and the school for young people and adults needing instruction. Besides the superintendent and the Pastor, the infant school needs but one teacher, though

assistants may often be usefully employed. This teacher
will ordinarily be a woman, but not necessarily. Men
are sometimes found, and ought to be, in most parishes,
with the necessary qualifications. This teacher must be a
Communicant, fond of children, one whom children will
instinctively love, able to talk to them, and interest them
in whatsoever is taught; one who can both sing and
teach singing; one competent in Bible history and the elements of Christian knowledge; one whose loving heart,
much more than brilliancy of intellect or wide learning,
can lead the young in the footsteps of the Child Jesus and
to His faith and love.

The Lord's Prayer, the Creed, and the Ten Command-
ments are the first things to be learned. They must be
taught *orally*, little by little. No reliance is to be placed
upon lessons being learned at home. Text books are not
essential. Simple catechisms are to be used as helps
explanatory of the chief things a child ought to know and
believe. The answers are to be taught *viva voce*, and
given, for the most part, in concert. Stories from the
Bible or other sources are subsidiary to the main object
and help to give variety and interest.

The devotional part must not be of secondary importance. The education of the heart is quite as important as
of the intellect. Collects from the Prayer Book and
special prayers for specific objects should be learned. The
Church canticles and good hymns should be committed

to memory. It should be a special aim to teach little children to appreciate, and love, and to join with their voices whenever practicable in the services of the House of God. The infant school must be furnished with all needful helps. An organ is very desirable. Catechisms, picture cards, papers for distribution, are necessary. Library books may be dispensed with. Few of this class of children can read. They learn first from example, and by the hearing ear. Then will come the understanding heart.

They are of all classes, but the poor and those of the self-respecting working class preponderate. They are gathered in by systematic visiting, and by all those nameless acts of kindness, which win their young hearts and gain the confidence of their parents. These are often brought into the Church through the instrumentality of their children, seconded by that of the teacher and district visitor and Pastor.

It is quite essential that the children should be baptized. The teaching, all pre-supposes that they are in the state of grace and salvation. The parents' consent must be given. No effort is to be spared to win the parents with the children, for until they are in the sphere of the grace and under the obligations of the Christian Covenant, the greatest power of teaching and influence over them and their children is lost.

The infant school ought to have a separate room, so

constructed that it can be opened into the larger school.
If this can not be provided, what can not be done in the
school must be done at the home of the teacher, superintendent or Pastor, or at other hours than those of the
general session of the school.

From the infant department the children pass into the
school of youth. Here, if possible, one uniform plan of
instruction is followed. It was common a few years since,
for some Pastors to work out for their own children a
complete course, and at the beginning of the year (Advent) to print a large card specifying the passages of
Scripture and the portions of the Church Catechism to be
learned by heart, with perhaps the Collect for the day;
and each week or month, to set forth, in print, if necessary, his own questions, references and answers in explanation, and himself personally teaching every lesson
beforehand to his own teachers. This is a great labor,
but if pursued with skill and diligence, cannot but be
rewarded. At present the leaflet system is in full vogue.
Doubtless this plan has its merits, such as uniformity of
lessons throughout the Church, the helps given to teachers who will study, the great amount of Scripture knowledge given; but it has its disadvantages also, except for
very advanced classes. The lessons are generally too long.
Few can commit them to memory, and it is exceedingly
important that all Scripture lessons, as well as the Catechism, should be accurately committed. The Word,

sown in good hearts, is sure ultimately to germinate and bring forth fruit. The knowledge gained is general, vague, indefinite. Too little attention is given to the Church Catechism. Too little is learned concerning the Church, its polity, history and ordinances. As we best learn any natural science, by using the labors of investigators who have collected and systematized the facts for us, and generalized their laws and principles, rather than by beginning anew, and without guidance, going out alone into the fields of nature in individual exploration, so we may best study the Holy Scriptures. The Church has formulated their essential facts and doctrines. In the Catechism, the elements of Christian doctrine and duty are set forth from the Scriptures in a form easily learned. Devout and able men have systematized the teachings of Scripture. We can only make real progress in the study of Christianity, by using the helps afforded us. It is only with these helps, as keys to interpretation, that we may hope to study the Bible with much profit. The common practice, therefore, of ranging at large through the whole Bible without system or definite aim will generally be unfruitful, while the learning by heart all that is possible of the *ipsissima verba* of Scripture, the Psalter, the Epistles and Gospels, the Memoirs of our Lord, the Acts, the Epistles, is exceedingly important. It is believed that the youth in the Sunday-school will make far better progress in learning the meaning of the Scriptures, and gain far more full and accurate knowledge of Christianity, by the use of catechisms, than by any leaflet system that has yet been devised.   There are many books of catechetical teaching from which to choose.   Of the older, Beavan's " Help to Catechizing " is most admirable ; Sadler's " Teachers' Manual " for teachers is still better, being more full and complete ; Maclear's " Class Book on the Church Catechism " is excellent.   The Bishop Doane series is one of the best, covering, as it does, the fundamental principles and facts of Scripture, doctrine, polity and history, though exception has been taken to some of its doctrinal statements.   Bishop Burgess' " Questions on the Gospels," the Witherspoon series, and others that might be named, are good and useful.   For very young children the " Calvary Catechism," and other like works, are interesting.   The teachers should be, if possible, members of the Church and communicants—ripe, well furnished, intelligent Christians. It is desirable that they should be parents having their own children in their classes.   The divorce of the Sunday-school from the family will thus be to some extent prevented.   Parents are better teachers, other things being equal, because they know more of the nature and wants of children, and feel more deeply their responsibilities. Others, however, if qualified, should not be excluded. Every lesson must be carefully studied by the teacher. Practical and Scripture illustrations should be found wherewith to impress and enforce the teaching.   Thus the lessons will be made interesting. If the parents be Christians, they will see that the lessons are thoroughly learned and understood, by requiring that they be first recited at home. Lessons well learned, so as to be well recited, give life, interest, enthusiasm to the exercises. Dullness in the teacher and in the pupils produces deadness in the school.

To qualify the teachers, there should be regular meetings for the study of the lessons, and for discussion of plans for increase of interest and success. These instructions should be attended not only by the best, most faithful teachers, who need them least, but by all, especially by those who have had little experience. These should be eager to attend and to profit by study and by the suggestions of the older and more experienced.

Catechizings by the Minister should be frequent. Parents and others of the congregation should attend, for the children's sake and their own. Their interest manifested in every way will deepen the interest of the children. They will find the instruction profitable for themselves, renewing their elementary knowledge and strengthening the foundations of first principles. Sermons should often have the children in view. If prepared so that children will understand them, most adults will be more interested and profited. It must not be forgotten that all adults are children though of larger growth.

A most indispensable requisite in those who conduct

Sunday-schools, is enthusiasm. They must be wide awake, full of life; without it there will be little interest. Enthusiasm is contagious; life produces life.

The Sunday-school is part of the Church, hence the devotional element must not be neglected. This is essential to the teaching. It subserves heart culture. It is a training of the regenerate nature. The best Liturgy, in the popular sense of the word, is the Prayer Book. For responsive worship, nothing is so good as the Psalter. It furnishes the most suitable "Psalms and Hymns and Spiritual Songs." Chanting may be made the most popular mode of singing. A whole school can easily be taught to sing chants with sufficient accuracy and with the greatest interest and enthusiasm. The Psalter, the Canticles, the Creed, Lord's Prayer, Versicles and Collects may be used with splendid effect. For variety, the Litany or the Ante-Communion, rendered chorally, may be effectively used. Additional prayers for specific objects, in which all are taught to feel an interest, should be added. Many a worthy end may be gained by the efficacy of the fervent prayers of faithful children. The use of the Prayer Book is made familiar. The chants and hymns are learned that are sung in Church. Hymns specially adapted to children are not necessary; they are apt to be puerile and sentimental. The Sunday-school should learn and use the very best, those that are worth learning, and will be always valued. The school is not dissociated from the

Church. The services must not be of a different character. To love it will be to love the Church. Children's hearts and voices will be attuned to the Church's worship, and the Sanctuary will be a delight. If on every Sunday afternoon, or at least monthly, the whole Sunday-school, after its usual lessons and exercises, could pass in procession, with their school and class banners, into the Church, and there join in a grand choral service, the Minister catechizing, as of old, after the Second Lesson, we should have doubtless the ideal plan. If the Pastor is the life of the Sunday-school, if he secures the love of every child, if he knows how to inspire zeal and enthusiasm, if he studies hard to master the art of catechizing, giving more time and labor to this work than to his sermons, he will doubtless succeed in realizing it.

The Festivals of the Church, especially Christmas and Easter, may be made delightful instrumentalities for promoting Christian teaching. Many of us have not yet learned all that might be made of a Christmas Festival for the Sunday-School, and Easter may be made quite as interesting and fruitful of enjoyment and of instruction as Christmas to teachers and scholars, in the work of the Sunday-school. These and other Church Festivals will be instinctively loved by every rightly instructed child.

It is a great mistake to suppose that children should not attend the Church as well as Sunday-school. There is no danger of fatigue, except in the case of the very young, or those in delicate health. They are not *confined* in the Church any more than in the Sunday-school. The changes of posture required in the services are restful. Standing, kneeling, sitting, at the proper times; singing, responding audibly, all this keeps up interest, and necessarily prevents fatigue. There will be no weariness, if real interest is cultivated and secured.

The original design of the Sunday-school should be kept prominent; the gathering in and teaching poor and vagrant children in pure religion and good manners. Systematic and thorough visiting is necessary. Children themselves, if imbued as they should be with the missionary spirit, will be able to render large assistance. All the teachers should spend a certain time each week in visiting their scholars at their homes, and gradually extending their influence to the surrounding masses; never yielding to discouragement, never relaxing effort, till all whom they seek are Church attendants and are brought effectively within the Church's influence. This work of visiting should be so distributed and so systematized that the power of the Church shall be felt for good in every street and suburb, and in every home. Even those who do not go with us will recognize this, and say that "the Lord is with us of a truth."

The Sunday-school fails of its end if many of those under its care are not brought to Confirmation and Holy Communion, and trained for the Christian life. How few realize their great responsibilities towards the young who may be gathered through the Sunday-school into the Flock of Christ!

There are many youth who ought to be in the Sunday-school who think themselves too old. Numbers of these are not attendants at Church; they have drifted out into the world. The smattering, superficial knowledge of Christianity they have gained, is assumed to be all there is to be known; they have tried it; they have had enough of it; it is of little account in their view; they have got beyond it and renounced it. That any should go out from the Sunday-school with such crude and shallow notions is a warning against attempting too much, and doing the work superficially. Nothing should be undertaken in the Sunday-school that can not be done thoroughly and well. But a great problem is suggested: how to prevent such youth leaving the Sunday-school prematurely in such fundamental ignorance of Christianity. Clearly there must be a higher department of study, of adults, both men and women, the youth, those of middle life; indeed, of all ages. In the School of Christ we never graduate. None should leave the Sunday-school before every effort is made to bring them to Confirmation. They who are not qualified to be teachers should remain as scholars. There should be Bible classes for all degrees of proficiency. How interesting and how profitable it would be, should the members of the congregation resolve themselves into classes for the study of Holy Scripture, the Prayer Book, Christian doctrine, Church history and polity under competent teachers, the Rector giving his assistance and co-operation.

Such classes may meet at the same time as the Sunday-school. It is desirable that they be parts of the Sunday-school, and hence there should be, when practicable, rooms contiguous, with folding doors, to be thrown into one for general exercises and services. The Church itself, however, may be best for such purposes. But it is well to have also separate meetings of the classes of this higher, as well as of the main department, in the parish building, at the Pastor's study, or in the homes of the teachers or some of the members. How much might be thus learned ! How pleasant it would be socially ! How closely it would tend to bind all hearts ! How deep an interest it would create in one another and in the Church of our love !

In forming and building up Bible classes in connection with the Sunday-school, we must never lose sight of the class of people who are as yet practically outside the Church, and in great ignorance of the Church and the Gospel; and who especially need, for themselves and their children, the refining, elevating, regenerating influences of Christianity. I refer to such of the great working class as have not been trained from their youth in the ways of godliness, or who, having been thus trained, have fallen back into the world; who make Sunday a work-day or a holiday, or a day of indolence or vice. Our strenuous efforts must be directed to gather in and Christianize their children. But we shall not succeed even with these, unless we go farther. It is our bounden duty to bring to bear upon all the adults of this class, the sanctifying influences of the Gospel. Experience has proved that they may be won to the Church. It would be invidious to mention examples. But there are instances in abundance, where it has been tried with great success in this country.

It has been proved by results that Christian women are peculiarly fitted for success in this good work. What they have already done almost surpasses belief to such as do not know their capabilities. I need but refer to their devoted missionary labors in the hospital, in the tent of the soldier, in the neglected parts of cities, among operatives in mills and factories; how they have displayed the beneficence of the Gospel, and proved the omnipotence of Christian love; how thousands of the rugged sons of toil have been taught of Him Who on earth had not where to lay His head; Who became poor to make the many rich. You have sources of information. Read, and ponder, and make the whole matter a subject of earnest prayer.

Women will succeed best with classes for men. Men and women should be in separate classes. I have seen in connection with one Sunday-school, classes of fifty, one hundred, and of one hundred and fifty or more, each class gathered and presided over and instructed by one earnest Christian woman; and this work going on year after year with increasing interest and success. Under less favorable circumstances there have been like classes of a dozen, or a score, or forty or fifty, with proportionately good results. The men were migratory, moving often for better wages. But the places of those leaving would be taken by others. Correspondence would be kept up with those who had gone elsewhere. The influence for good gained over the men and their families would be lifelong.

Not the Bible class only, but the cottage lecture, conducted by the clergyman or by a devout layman, for men and women, and the Mothers' Meeting, and the Sewing-school for women and girls, conducted each by a good woman with her assistants, with indefatigable, systematic visiting, are means of wonderful efficacy in themselves, and in their indirect influence in building up the Sunday-school, and the congregation.

Of course, the objection occurs to all such efforts, that they would take much time and absorb much of the thought and energies of Christian people. But who can suppose that real Christian character is evidenced merely by Church attendance on Sundays and perfunctory gifts of money that cost no thought nor pains? Who can suppose that we can fulfill our Christian duty and meet our obligations in the Church by proxy? Is not Christian work the *business* of Christians? Consider the Church's Charter, by virtue of which she exists. The Apostles distributed their work of preaching the Gospel to every creature and discipling all nations. The threefold Ministry is in the place of leadership. The great body of the faithful must stand behind and with them in earnest co-operation. The work is yours. You must do it, if you be not recreant to all Christian vows and obligations.

IV.

Psalm cxlviii, 12, 13: Both young men and maidens, old men and children, let them praise the name of the Lord.

THE Psalmist calls upon all people of all ages, classes and conditions to praise the name of the Lord. Praise is here to be taken as inclusive of every kind of worship. Worship is necessarily public. It is not worship on special and extraordinary occasions that is referred to. It is stated, regular, habitual. It is the outward expression of the inward feelings of the heart rightly disposed. It is the open recognition of God's greatness, and power, and wisdom, and love. It is not so much to ask as to give. "Honor great our Lord befitteth." "Unto Him be glory in the Church by Christ Jesus throughout all ages, world without end. Amen."

True worship unites all hearts and voices. It cannot be individual only. It cannot be extemporarily framed. It must be the voice of the Church. It is the result of pre-arrangement and concert. It necessarily involves a religious training, that it may be done so as to subserve its great purpose of honoring God, as is His due, with the sacrifices of our lips expressing the devotion of our hearts and of all our members. To render such a service of worship to God manifestly requires earnest thought, study and teaching.

Worship was secured in the Jewish Dispensation by the Temple services, and later also to some extent in the Synagogue. In the Christian Dispensation it is secured by the Christian services which have grown up in the various branches of the historic Church, according to Apostolic norm and precedents, under Episcopal direction and oversight, and conciliar enactment. The Liturgy proper, which is the office of the Holy Communion, has come down to us in different families, each family preserving through the ages its distinctive family type, but varying largely in accordance with the spiritual and intellectual tone and spirit of the peoples using it, in successive ages. Our own is the Reformed Gallican, which is Johannine or Ephesian in origin. The offices for daily Morning and Evening Prayer have grown in like manner from early types, their modifications and transformations in the course of history not affecting the character of their essential elements; the use of the Psalter, Versicles, Lessons from the Old and New Testament, the Evangelical

Hymns, the Creed, the Lord's Prayer, being constant through all mutations.

Our national Church has its own Use, both in the Liturgy, and Matins and Even Song, as well as other offices. In respect of fulness of Scripture, accuracy of catholic teaching and freedom from doctrinal or practical error, we are better provided for than any Church in the world.

Wherever the Church plants Christianity, she gathers her congregations in parishes and missions, and establishes public services, and trains her converts to their devout, intelligent use. This training in the use of the offices of worship is so very important, that it is required to be begun in the earliest years from the time the baptized child is made conscious of its Church relations, and carried on through youth and manhood. Constant use confirms devout habits. Christian life finds its fit expression in the hallowed services of the sanctuary. True worship has a wonderful educational influence. The best training in the Christian life is impossible without it. It is intended to be the antetype of the heavenly worship, and to prepare us therefor. We must begin here if we would be qualified there, to sing the "Song of Moses and the Lamb."

The parish or mission is organized to bring men to Christ in membership of His Church, and then to edify and train them to render acceptable service to God. The parish or mission in any place, theoretically embraces

all the souls within its limits who do not disown it.
Practically, it embraces all who can be brought under its
influences. All who are not gathered in Christian bodies,
not of the Communion of the Church, are the proper subjects of the parochial or mission work. "Young men and
maidens, old men and children," who are outside of the
pale of Christianity, as organized in some form or other,
whether they be living in unbelief or indifference, are to
be sought out, and by every effort that can be prompted
by the love of Christ and of souls, are to be won to Him,
brought into the corporate life of Christianity, and trained
in holy worship, and fitted for the heavenly citizenship
and its employments.

The question now is, as to the mode and agencies by
which men and women, young and old, rich and poor, can
be led to join with heart and voice in the stated, habitual
worship required in the Church of Christ, and be trained
thereby in the spiritual life.

The Clergy should feel that upon them rests the highest degree of responsibility in bringing about such result.
They are to set forth the Scripture teaching on this subject. They are to show that all people are called upon
by every consideration to worship God, and to praise the
Lord with the voice, and with the mind and soul, and all
the members. They are to strive earnestly to win them
to this delightful employment, and show the ways in
which the Church, after the example of Christ, teaches

them how to pray. Publicly and privately they are to set
forth its blessings, and recommend and enforce their
teaching by their example. In establishing missions and
new congregations, it is well to make a business of instructing the people in the use of the Prayer Book, in
"finding the places," and making the responses. Meetings are held for this purpose, and for practice in chanting. Such exercises will be found interesting in themselves, and will tell wonderfully upon the heartiness and
effectiveness of the services.

The Clergy must be leaders in this, as in all other
teaching and work. But what can the brethren do? How
can all Christian people of our congregations lend their
aid in training people of all ages, ranks and conditions, to
unite intelligently and heartily in the public service of
prayer and praise?

The Church has set forth a service admirably adapted
to the end in view. It is interesting in itself. It is full
of Gospel truth. For the instruction of the ignorant, no
other form of service can be compared with it. Let these
prayers and praises, these Creeds and hymns, these Scripture lessons, and the teaching with which they are full, be
well stored in the memory by habitual use, and the worshipper is thoroughly furnished as to all needful doctrine
and duty. The most illiterate, by constant attendance in
the Church, by devout attention, joining in the words as
heard and remembered, will soon be able to unite verbally

as well as heartily in all those parts in which the tongue is called upon to express the inward devotion. Many who could not read have been in this way taught, with the same effect as when John the Baptist and our Lord, after his example, taught His disciples to pray. They have learned the true objects of prayer, praise and thankgiving. They have gained the inspiration for worship, and have found the fittest expressions therefor, which, without such instruction, had been beyond their attainment.

Consider, too, the great variety in the service. With its many parts, each in its due place, it forms a complete, harmonious whole. Nothing could be well omitted. Nothing needs to be added to make it better subserve its purpose. Whether it be the Morning or Evening Prayer, or the Litany, or the Holy Communion, each is in itself complete. No attentive, unprejudiced worshipper can look upon it as bald or unattractive, if there be that warmth of devotion in its reading which is requisite. It is lack of that familiarity which comes of study of it and training in its use that makes it appear so to any. Those who rightly use it, it can never weary. Familiarity only discloses new fitnesses and new beauties. With every repetition it becomes dearer. It is hallowed by the sacred memories of the past. It is associated with loved ones of whom the thought is precious. As when you hear some old hymn, of which the words and tune were caught from the mother's voice in childhood, in which father and mother and brothers and sisters, now separated perhaps by death, joined with glad hearts around the hearth and at the altar of prayer, you are carried back to the happy days of youth, and in the old familiar scenes of home are joined in spirit with the departed; so in the dear old service of the House of God, giving yourself up to the inspiration by which thought and devotion are quickened, entering into full sympathy with the spirit of the words, and the influences of the gathered associations of years, thoughtless of self and of the world without, time and space are annihilated; associated with you are Martyrs and Confessors, Fathers and Reformers, and those whom you have known and loved are with and around you. You realize the glorious Communion of the Saints in Christ. You *** with them in the heavenly places. This is particularly so as you join in the service of the Holy Communion, the principal service of the Lord's Day.

Such experiences are especially for those who were taught to love the service by the precept and example of paternal love and piety, whose kindred have loved it, and whose ancestry in a long line have equally loved it, and have been fitted by its use for Heaven. Still there are none to whom it does not, rightly used, become more loved, more sacred, and more effective. To all it is a glorious service, fitted, as well as it can be, to engage the heart, to instruct the understanding, and to assist with the greatest effectiveness in the preparation for the worship of

Heaven itself, the perpetual joy of the Saints perfected. If we set aside the Bible, of which it is so full, and to the understanding of which it is the best key, the Prayer Book is the richest treasure we inherit from the past. We should not be without safe guidance in faith and duty were all else of Holy Scripture lost to us.

The Church has done her part. No forms of words could be better adapted to train persons of whatever class to a devout, hearty and intelligent worship. But there are conditions of its effectiveness. It must not by the Minister only, but by the people, be properly rendered. It must be the channel for the devotions of living, loving hearts, united by the electric chords of interest and sympathy. Its responsive utterances must be warm from hearts that have been quickened by the Spirit of Christ. The whole soul of the worshipper must speak in every word that comes from the lips. The full AMEN must be the heart's endorsement of every petition.

Now, the suggestions to be made are not theoretical, but might be reduced to immediate practice. It is not the purpose to give merely a beautiful picture of what might be and ought to be ultimately realized in every worshipping assembly, but a plain statement of what is practicable and necessary to the end proposed, which is the training of both young men and maidens, old men and children, of every class, to intelligent and cordial worship. It is the duty and privilege of all who are, or who can be incorporated into the fellowship of the Church, that is to be set forth.

Suppose, then, that you come regularly to service, never defrauding the Lord of any part of the sacred time, the morning and evening of the Lord's Day, and the Holy Days and Seasons appointed for your observance. You bring your children, all who are old enough to lisp the name of Jesus and to say "Our Father." You bring, if possible, your man servants and maid servants, if such you have, for their souls are as precious as your own, and you are, to some extent, responsible for their religious training. They sit with you in the same or contiguous seats, for all are equal in the House of God; and the Church does not obliterate, but sanctions and hallows the family relationships. The congregation is made up of families as such, with the individuals not thus included, all contributing to form the larger family of God. So, too, you bring all others whom you can reach. You go out into the highways and compel all you can influence to come in, that God's House may be full. All the men and women, if any, in your employ; the laborers, if any, in your fields, in your mines, in your manufactories and stores. It is required of you that they shall keep and hallow the Lord's Day, and by your intercourse with them, you have won them, some of them, at least, to appreciate and love its holy services. So, too, your friends; those whom you often meet in society, those with whom you have busi-

ness relations, those with whom you are in frequent intercourse; all, in short, who come within the sphere of your
influence, are to be attracted, persuaded and led, by all
the means God has given you to use, to share with you the
privileges of the Lord's Day and the Lord's House.
You will, of course, fail to bring as many as you would.
There are other influences counteracting your efforts; there
are many adversaries. But you will bring some; you may
bring many by judicious persistence in the effort. They
are mingled in the congregation with a total oblivion, for
the time being, of all class distinctions. The seats are all
free, though families and individuals sit in their accus-
tomed places. None can have any property rights in
God's House. All are supplied with Prayer Books and
Hymnals. All have been instructed in the order of
service. You have explained beforehand its purpose
and meaning. All now must find a voice. All hearts
in whom is God's Spirit are attuned to worship. There
is no time for languor or inattention. The mind must
be intensely active, compelling earnest attention, and
taking home the full import of the words of prayer and
praise. The affections must be kindled with living fire,
as if every heart were touched with a burning coal from
off God's altar. A warming, enlivening influence will go
forth from every true worshipper, pervading the holy
place. Few can remain indifferent. They will catch
something of the inspiration. There will be no waiting

for the Minister to indicate when to kneel for prayer, nor for the organ to give the reminder to rise and join in the praises. There will be no gazing about, no whispered conversation. All true Christians will be intent upon their work. The responses will be made in full, audible tones, instinct with the impulse and power of devotion. Children's voices will be heard with those of men and women, all in a grand, sonorous unison. No single voice will be distinguished; all voices will blend; each contributing to the power and volume of sound with which Heaven's gates are assaulted; and the Spirit of God will descend as in cloven tongues of fire upon the head of each, as on the First Pentecost. Few can resist the impulse to join in such worship. As in the primitive assemblies at Corinth, "if there come in one that believeth not, or one that is unlearned, he is convinced of all; he is judged of all, and thus the secrets of his heart are made manifest. And so falling down on his face, he will worship God and report that God is in you of a truth."

Something should be said of the singing which will render the praises of the Church most interesting and most effective. Nobody can contend for "operatic" music without first forgetting or ignoring its purpose. The Canticles and "Psalms, and Hymns, and Spiritual Songs" are not to be listened to, not for display. "Let all the people praise God." Better have no choir at all than one that would take the words of common praise out of the mouths of the people by rendering it impossible for them to join in it. There must be no trills, no notes for which there is no place, no useless slurs, no superfluous quavers and semi-quavers; the words must be spoken out in clear, full tones in a grand melody to which all can contribute. There should be no drawling; chanting and singing should be quick, lively, spirited, imparting life instead of weariness and lassitude. The veriest children should be encouraged and taught to sing. To the youngest members of the congregation the service may thus be made marvellously attractive. They will love it enthusiastically and their delight in it will grow with their years. The choir may, indeed, have its anthem, provided it be worthy. No music can be too grand and lofty for God's service. But every choir must be taught its place. Its office is not to appropriate, but to lead the people's praises.

If you are to have congregational singing you must have congregational practice. The Sunday-school can do much to promote it. In many places the best choir to be had would be formed of all the best singers in the Sunday-school; and they would take delight in the practice necessary, if properly conducted. But all the people who sing in the congregation might be often called together for so delightful an exercise. The leader, with the help of the organ, might so instruct all willing learners, that they could chant and sing the best tunes, such as ought to be made familiar, with such correctness and such spirit that the musical part would be rendered with a simplicity and grandeur of which you now have little conception.

Besides the endeavors each member of the congregation must feel it to be an imperative duty to make, to invite, persuade, and win the people who are without to attend the services of the Church, there should be *organized effort*. Systematic visiting to this end is requisite. Bands should be formed to call regularly at every house, through all the streets and precincts, with the loving invitation to come to the service. The St. Andrew's Brotherhood, or some similar organization of men, will be found to be a most invaluable help. It is composed of the young men, who are each admitted by taking a solemn pledge to bring, each, some one person at least, to every service, and to pray for the extension of Christ's Kingdom. So the congregation, Sunday-school, Bible classes, schools, and agencies of various sorts are to be built up. By the harmonious action of all who are interested, the Church will be enlarged, and the "Word of God will grow mightily and prevail."

So we may gather in the people, young men and maidens, old men and children, those who live by the labor of their hands, and of their brains, making all of equal importance, all essential in the congregation. Thus we shall make it truly a worshipping assembly, realizing the idea of the popular hymnodist:

"Lord, how delightful 'tis to see,
A whole assembly worship Thee ;
At once they sing, at once they pray,
They hear of Heaven and learn the way."

The result of such efforts would be marvellous. The spirit of worship diffuses itself resistlessly. There are no listeners, no spectators. If any come to scoff they will remain to pray. Worship would assume its true place in the Church. It would be no longer a mere preliminary to preaching. Souls would be converted. The Church would be edified. Living stones would take their places, polished and bright, in the spiritual temple. It would be, in truth, the building of God.

It would be a delight to preach to such a congregation. They would hear only to learn. The matter would be more important than the manner. They would grow by the sincere milk of the Word. They would soon relish the strong meat, and digest and incorporate it into their spiritual fibre. They would become strong to labor for Christ and the Church.

But, alas, how far we are from doing our duty and realizing our privileges ! In how many of our congregations such work is not even begun ! Vainly we expect our churches to be filled and our people trained to worship, and the many without to come of their own accord to worship with us, without any effort on our part to bring them. Look around you in your Church. Your children are

not there. Your domestics and servants are not there.
The laboring classes are but poorly represented. The vast
multitudes to whom the Gospel is to be preached, where
they are you know not, but they are not with you in the
Church. O, how much we have to learn! When will we
conceive adequately our responsibility towards the poor,
perishing souls around us? When will we understand
that all souls bought by the precious blood of Christ are
as dear to Him as our own; that the only aristocracy in
the sight of God is one of virtue and piety, and that we
can only belong to it as we give and work, according to
our ability, for Christ and the salvation of men?

V.

Prov. xi, 25: He that watereth shall be watered also himself.

THERE is a certain type of piety which involves danger to Christian character. It is based upon a theory which claims to be evangelical, but which is without New Testament or Apostolic sanction. It makes much of repentance, conversion of the heart to God, reliance on the Atonement and the finished work of Christ, and is so far right; but it stops there. It distrusts everything outward. It puts Christ and the Church, heart religion and working religion, the soul and the body of Christianity, in antagonism. It speaks of the outward and visible in the Gospel, as the husk or shell of religion, as if it were of no account; as if the Kingdom of Christ were dead; as if the Institution of Christianity, the Body of Christ, were not living by Christ's own life through His Spirit, growing in the world and maturing the fruits of righteousness. The full corn in the ear cannot grow and be matured without its living, outward envelopment. The shell in the whole process of growth, is part of the living organism by which the life-germ in the acorn reaches its maturity. Life everywhere is dependent upon the organism; separate it therefrom and it is but an abstraction. It is only an outward, visible, organic thing that lives. The organism is essential to the life. If Christianity be vital, it must be through the organism that embodies it. Works must manifest inward faith. Life must be seen in its activities. The Gospel of Christ is the Gospel of the Kingdom. As a system of doctrines merely, making its own way as best it might, Christianity would be inoperative. It is Christianity organized and working, showing the fruits of life, it is the corporate vitality of Christ's own Institution, that is to reform and save the world. We must be organically, vitally in the Body of Christ, and each one of us must live and act out its life. So we grow up into Christ, the Head of the Body. So we get grace and grow in grace.

It is a great first principle of the divine economy, announced in every variety of form throughout the Holy Scriptures, that "he that watereth shall be watered also himself." Like all great truths, it has its negative as well as positive side. He who neglects this duty, shall find drought and barrenness in his own soul. He who declines to work for Christ, for His Church and for the best good of his fellow men, though apparently in all else an exemplary Christian, is not only unprofitable, but is in

himself worthless. He fails to get grace through the cus-
tomary channels. He is in the Church what the barren
fig-tree is in the field. He is an encumbrance rather
than a blessing. But he who does not forget to do good
and to communicate of his own store, which God has
given him, whether of gifts or labors; who delights in
words and acts of kindness, by which to show the spirit of
his Master; who makes the cause of Christ and the Church
his own, working therefor as zealously and self-denyingly
as, under any circumstances, he would work for himself,
receives far richer blessing than he can bestow. While he
scatters, he increases. He reaps thirty, sixty and an hun-
dredfold more than he sows. He saves his life by sacri-
ficing it. It is of him it is said, "To him that hath shall
be given, and he shall have abundance." So it is of the
Parish, and of the Diocese, and of the Church in the
Nation.

The cultivation of such a spirit in every individual
member of the Church is, therefore, a necessity. It is the
true missionary spirit. With it a parish is almost omnip-
otent for good. Without it, it does little more than add
one to the catalogue of Churches.

What are our defects in this regard? What are the
modes by which this missionary spirit can be cultivated?

When we say that there is much too little missionary
life and zeal among us, we make a statement which few
will be disposed to question. Most of our parishes work

chiefly, almost exclusively, for themselves. And their highest aim would seem to be their temporal, financial prosperity. There are, indeed, many notable exceptions. There are congregations of the Church all over the land in which the evident desire and purpose is to give and work to the extent of the ability God giveth for the salvation and edification of others. In every congregation there are some who are alive to missionary duty. But the vast majority of professing Christians in the Church do not seem to be adequately conscious of the obligations resting upon them, and the fearful responsibilities they are neglecting.

Our Church has again and again proclaimed herself in her highest Council, a missionary society, and declared that every Christian is a member. Never was there a truer or nobler declaration of privilege and duty. But how few seem to be aware of this great fact. How few enter into this spirit. How few act as if they knew and felt themselves to be missionaries. Is it not the idea of most of us that a missionary is one who goes into a foreign land, or into wilderness regions to preach the Gospel to the heathen? Or that he is a missionary who receives his support wholly, or in part, from some Board of Missions, Diocesan or General? Did it never occur to you that Jesus Christ was the first and greatest missionary? That every one of the Apostles was a missionary? That all the Ministers of the Apostolic and early Church were missionaries? That the same was true of all the Christians of the Apostolic and the primitive ages? That they all believed themselves to be missionaries, and lived, and acted upon this presumption? Why should it be different now? Why is not every Minister, wherever laboring, a missionary? Why is not every Christian? Why not you? Every man, woman and child who has received the grace of God, in Christ, in membership of His Body, who loves the Saviour, and prays for the extension of His Kingdom?

But the common theory has been the contradictory of this truth. Hence our great practical deficiencies. Our people not having been taught and not feeling that they are missionaries, have not actually been such. The members failing in this primary duty, the Body of Christ has failed to make increase in anything like the measure that ought to be expected. Our Church to-day is only ministering to a fraction of the people. Denominations that have nothing like our wealth or our social advantages, and whose instrumentalities of effort, as compared with ours, are extremely defective, would seem to be surpassing us in missionary zeal. They exhibit more *esprit du corps.* They support more loyally their own schools and other institutions. They have the most implicit faith in their imperfect systems. Faith is the inspiration of effort. Confidence brings success. They give and work with unselfish devotion, and God blesses them. They are constantly anticipating us and doing work that is incumbent upon us. Till of late years they entered almost every new field before us. We had to glean where they had gathered the harvest. It is doubtless true that our Church on the whole is making greater progress than any of the denominations referred to. The work that is really done with us tells more. We organize and teach, and hold better what we gain. Our Apostolic and catholic system is an inestimable advantage. But it must be worked by living persons. It will not work itself. So far as we are not of its spirit we are but parasites upon its life, and it is barren and unfruitful.

We have, thank God, among our laity some true missionaries—some among our male, many more among our female membership. What progress the Church is making is largely due to these. The seal of God has been set upon their ministries. The success which has crowned their labors shows how grand and glorious might be the triumphs of the Church if all would unite for similar efforts. They do what they can. They are pained that they can do no more. They need to be reinforced by the whole body of communicants, even by every member. Look around you, in the community you live in. How many of both adults and children, whose antecedents would lead them to the Church, who are not spiritually incorporated into her membership! How many there are who have fallen away from all direct religious influence, and for whom no religious body is caring! If we could get the statistics of all who, without reasonable excuse, keep away from all public worship, we should be surprised and alarmed at the number. In the West it is greater than at the East. It is to be feared that in many parishes public opinion is condoning, if not justifying, the use of the Lord's Day for drives and dinner parties and secular recreations. Young men who go out from Christian homes and associations and fall under the influence of this intense secularism and worldliness, are in the greatest peril. With so little to restrain and hold them to the Church, and the devout habits of Christian living, what wonder is it that so many of them fall? What wonder that so many of them, having become neglectful and non-religious, come to justify themselves by scepticism and denial of the truth of Christianity? What a work is before us, even at our own doors!

And then when we think of the call upon the Church for evangelizing labor in the country around us, in the great West and in the New West; in the poorer dioceses, with their teeming populations; in the missionary jurisdictions, where great empires are being born, which are going to be more important factors than we are apt to think, in determining the weal and the destinies of the nation; when we think of the foreign fields and the imperative demands of the foreign work, if we have the least sense of our responsibility, we ought to be filled with shame that we are doing so little ; we ought to see to it at once that the whole working capacity and strength of the Church shall be put in requisition ; we ought to be aroused to immediate and most determined action, to be pursued with the most unremitting zeal and energy, and to the fullest extent of our ability.

In excuse for negligence, the proverb is often quoted, that "charity begins at home." Would that it might! If it would only *begin* in the hearts of all who profess to belong to Christ! If we could see the manifestation of that highest charity which would give the Gospel to those who are perishing without it ; if it would but begin to prompt us to do to others what right feeling would prompt us to desire, if in their circumstances, they should do to us, there would surely be no fear of its ending. The work would be progressive, cumulative. Not only "at home," but all around us, and so far as we could extend our influence or our help, the "Word of God would have free course and be glorified," and "grow mightily and prevail."

There is a great truth that stands clearly revealed in God's Word, and is confirmed by all just reasoning, and everybody would admit it on its being once clearly pointed out. It is, that ability of every sort—intelligence, wealth, social position, and advantages—is a stewardship. It needs to be pressed home upon all people possessing such gifts that God has bestowed them as means of greater influence, and that they only heighten His claim for personal service. The pulpit must speak out upon this subject. A public opinion ought to be created that would constrain Christians of position in the community to use faithfully all the influence their standing and attainments give them, for the good of others and the advancement of the cause of Christ. He calls them *to work* in His vineyard. He has given them all they have. Their intelligence, wealth or standing in the world are intended to increase their usefulness, their power for good among their fellow men. It is easy to see how much more effective would be their personal labors from the possession of these advantages. They might wield a mighty influence for Christ and the Church, if they would only make it their predominant aim. There are no considerations that can excuse them from the responsibilities of this stewardship.

But most of the Christians of the class referred to, as judged by their lives, are totally oblivious of any obligation resting upon them for personal service in the cause of Christianity. They seem to think that pecuniary contributions, large or small, will purchase exemption from active duty, and that nothing more can be required. The general feeling among this class everywhere evidently is, that it is enough to attend Church of the Sunday morning, to bestow their mites at collections, and to assist in raising the Rector a salary, the amount of which is determined, too often, not by what is justly due him, not by what his learning and talents would earn for him in another profession, but what he can be compelled to live on by an enforced frugality and economy. Thus they regard themselves as in good and regular standing. They practically repel all further claims. If the parish is spiritually prosperous, if souls are gathered in and saved and edified, if the spiritual work which is the reason of the existence of the parish, is done, it must be by efforts not theirs, and to which they in no manner contribute. Who does not see that their position is wrong? Nothing could be more false to the teaching and spirit of Christianity. Personal, active co-operation in the work of the Church is what is required of them. The vows of their baptism, the grace of their confirmation, pledge them to this. By nothing else can they fulfill their bounden duty. They, as well as all others, must "have a mind " to work. In proportion as they have received, so must they freely give.

There is another great truth to be much insisted on. It is equally clear on its statement. All Christian people would do well to ponder it, to lay it to heart, and govern themselves accordingly. It is, that working for Christ naturally results in giving for His cause, while giving does not necessarily result in working. The working should be first. It is of primary importance. It is indispensable to lively interest. The heart becomes interested, when the mind and the will have aroused the active energies. Desire of success, of accomplishing the ends aimed at, will lead to prayer for strength to labor, and the divine response to the prayer. The prayer of faith, and work in faith, meet at a point and become identical. Giving will be from the right principle. It will be for the accomplishment of that for which we are working. It will be liberal. It will be such as to involve sacrifice. It will be with a cheerful heart. It will avail, because it costs something. Work and prayer will attend the giving, and the blessing of God will follow it.

It should be, then, the great object of every Minister and of every Christian, to promote in all a thorough missionary spirit, by leading them to work, to pray, to give, to spend and be spent, for the great end of saving souls, and extending and strengthening the Church of Christ.

We must begin with the children in the Sunday-school; earlier even than this, in the family. All our youth should be taught, by precept and example, the blessedness of doing good, of making sacrifices for others, of not only serving God themselves, but promoting His service among their companions, by being always kind, loving and unselfish. But it is in the Sunday-school that children come consciously under the influence of the parochial life. Here there should be special teaching, such as will promote habits of active usefulness, and foster the missionary spirit. The Sunday-school should be, in fact, a missionary society, led by the Pastor, superinten-

dent, and teachers.   In the school, as a whole, and in the
several classes into which it is subdivided, there should
be a corporate missionary life.   This is realized to some
extent in respect to contributions.   The school, in general,
and the separate classes, have their respective treasurers,
and there is a wholesome emulation in giving, as in other
duties.   Every Lord's day each child is supposed to give
to Christ His portion, which otherwise might be selfishly
hoarded or spent.   At stated times, monthly, or according
to the plan adopted, the several classes pour all their gifts
into the general treasury, and they are dedicated to God
upon His altar.   Especially should this be done on the
great Festival of the Children on Easter Day.   The educational influence of such a system is invaluable.   All, from
their youth, are familiarized with the idea of giving to
God.   The duty is thoroughly impressed, as it is thus
practically fulfilled.   The habit is formed which, like all
other habits of youth, especially when strengthened by
long continuance, will generally last through life.   Well
had it been for all of us if we had had such a training.
The treasury of the Church would be ample for every
demand, made necessary by her growing exigencies.   Frequent collections would be rejoiced in as opportunities for
testifying our gratitude to Him from Whom we receive
all we have, and the weekly offertory for outside missionary objects would be demanded by public sentiment.   We
should feel that we can never do too much for Him Who

hath redeemed us by the offering of His own life. We ought, therefore, to cherish a system which is intended to educate a generation of Christians who are soon to take our places, and who, in this regard, will be far more worthy to fill them.

But, as already shown, giving is secondary to working. Not only in the Sunday-school, but in the congregation, of which the Sunday-school is a part, the Church people should be made to feel a deep interest in the objects for which they give. Their feelings being enlisted, their prayers will be called forth and offered in faith, and they cannot but work for the attainment of the objects that are dear to them.

The missionary field begins in their very midst. How many there are all about us whom the love of Christ and of the work for which He came, should prompt and energize every Christian to strive to bring to Him in the Church, in which are the channels of His grace and blessings! The field should be gradually extended, as the needs are apprehended, to wider and wider circles, and as it is made apparent that the requirements of the Diocese are not secondary, and the Church of the Nation has also primary claims upon our allegiance and fealty. The intelligent, well-instructed Christian, who is really doing the missionary work of the local centre, will soon learn to recognize the great fact which the Gospel assumes, that no part of the world is outside the field in which the Church is appointed to labor.

Every member of the congregation should be taught to esteem rightly the Church's benefits to themselves, to the community they live in, to the country of which they are citizens. They cannot but feel the motives which should strongly actuate them to extend these benefits and to make others partakers of them. The Christian, duly esteeming his privileges and actuated by the convictions which his whole training in the Church must produce, cannot be true to himself, nor feel that he is faithful to trusts and responsibilities the most sacred, unless he become an active, efficient missionary and worker for Jesus Christ.

Success is God's gift. But as sure as He is true it will follow. And there are obvious reasons for the position that Christian laymen may succeed in gathering in the masses of people who are without, to membership of the congregation, and participation in many of the privileges and blessings of the Church. They are more in touch with all classes than the Clergy. They get from their more familiar intercourse with them, more intimate knowledge of their habits of thought and feeling. They can approach them when a Clergyman could not reach them. The fact of a man's being a Clergyman is enough to lead many people to avoid him. The earnest layman will have no such difficulty to overcome. He must be bold for Christ and earnest in this duty, and he will easily find opportunities, to bring before men of all classes with whom he is in constant association, and in a manner that shall attract and not repel them, the great subject of personal religion, and Church attendance, and membership.

Not only Sunday-school teachers, but the brethren who can not be connected with the Sunday-school, must do what they can to build up the congregation. They should seek out the absent, those whom they have invited to come and who have not availed themselves as yet of the privilege ; those who have not been connected with the Church, or have fallen out of all Church relations. They will patiently remove excuses, and by loving interest and persuasion " compel them to come in that God's House may be filled."

There is no class of Christians who cannot participate in such missionary work. Children may bring in children to Sunday-school and Church. Young men should be employed as ushers, and in other ways in and about the Church. In such societies as the St. Andrew's Brotherhood, they may be strengthened in their Christian purposes by being pledged to bring each some one person to every service, and to pray for the prosperity of the parish and the Church. Most persons, when any are sick or in affliction, can not only themselves give some personal attendance, relief or comfort, but can " call for the Elders of the Church," who will always be at hand with the authoritative ministrations of the Gospel. Christian women, not only as organized in sisterhoods, but whose duties are chiefly in their families and in society, can accomplish much by visiting regularly in convenient districts under pastoral direction, in bringing people to Church, ministering to the sick, bringing comfort to the afflicted, instructing and helping many souls in their Christian living. What opportunities may not be found by all Christian people, to exert some positive Christian influence in keeping up interest in the Church and in her Missions, in promoting religion among their companions, in rebuking profanity and vice, and imparting of their Christian knowledge, wherever there is a call for words fitly spoken, without obtrusiveness or the violation of obvious proprieties.

One thing especially should not be neglected. Boys who are fond of study should be led to entertain the question whether they are not called of God to prepare for the sacred Ministry. Every parish ought to be able to furnish recruits year by year for the Clerical ranks. If parents, pastors and teachers would frequently call the attention of the young to the matter, and impress upon them the duty of self-examination in reference to this work, large numbers of young men, who would otherwise enter upon secular avocations, would doubtless be led to engage in this holy calling as the profession and work of their lives. Many Christian parents should dedicate their sons to the Ministry from their baptism, and educate them with reference thereto. It is in such ways that the Holy Spirit gives the call, and the knowledge and consciousness of the call, and prompts obedience thereto. Many are to-day in the Ministry from such a dedication in infancy, and a godly mother's teaching and prayers.

There is not time nor need to point out in detail all the missionary work that should enlist the sympathies and active co-operation of every one individually of the men and women of the parish. They whose hearts are in the work will find their appropriate spheres of labor in connection with the Sunday-school, district visiting, the parish societies and guilds, sewing-schools for girls, cottage lectures, clubs for men, mothers' meetings for women. Why should not the Vestry undertake, in earnest co-operation with the Rector, the work of increasing attendance at Church, looking up, visiting, introducing and otherwise showing acceptable attention to strangers, bringing to Church the poor and the working classes, and, in general, promoting the enlargement and edification of the congregation, and the meeting fully of all missionary obligations for the Diocese and the Church at large, not forgetting the great field which is the world, thus helping to build up the spiritual edifice as well as those interests that are material in their nature.

But we must not forget in all our plans for building up the Church, that there is no possible substitute for spiritual life. This cannot be produced by organization, however perfect. Life is organic and results in growth. Life is first. This is the universal law. Unless we have the life of Christ and are constrained to effort by His love, all our schemes will be in vain.

VI

ON THE NECESSITY AND THE MODES OF PROMOTING CHRIS-
TIAN FELLOWSHIP IN THE CHURCH.

Romans xii, 16: Be of the same mind, one towards
another. Mind not high things, but condescend to men
of low estate.

THE critical exposition of these words is not necessary.
It is their obvious meaning I wish to enforce. They
require an intimate communion of all Christians, one
with another. They require that such communion and
fellowship be unrestricted. Class distinctions must not
be allowed to limit it. The high-born and the lowly, the
rich and the poor, must meet together in loving intercourse, for God is the Maker of them all, and Christ
Jesus, the Saviour, has redeemed them. The words
plainly say to us: "Let yourself down to the wretched.
Withdraw not from the poor and despised, who as yet
know not the Gospel." Self-withdrawal and exclusiveness
belong to the religion of the Old Testament. The New
Testament requires communion of all who partake of its
spirit, even with those in whom the life of Christ does not
yet bear sway. The proverb, "tell me what company you

keep, and I will tell you who you are," is, therefore, true only in the Old Testament, where exclusiveness was a duty. The Son of God teaches the faithful to consort with publicans and sinners, in order to win them for His Kingdom.

It must be obvious that in a well-worked parish provision should be made for the social element in our nature. Human distinctions belong to the world. We admit it in words, we must hold in fact, that in Christ Jesus rich and poor, masters and servants, stand on a perfect equality before God. It follows that individuals of all classes should be socially combined in the Church, and that there should be an intimate, real fellowship among them on the basis of Christian love.

It is clear from the text, and from many other like passages, that S. Paul proposed such an inward and vital union and its practical realization so that it should be seen and known of all men, between those of whatsoever outward conditions, who love, or may be brought to love, the Lord Jesus Christ. The whole life of the Saviour illustrates the value of such union of sympathy and affection, and shows how its necessity is laid in the very nature of Christianity. It was only as He sought the lost, and consorted with publicans and sinners, and found among the lowly His intimate and trusted friends, and won from the laboring classes His first Apostles, that He laid the foundation of His Kingdom.

Is there no lesson for us in the fact that under the influence of the Pentecostal gifts all worldly distinctions were for the time obliterated, and the ideal society of perfect Christian communion was realized, while all were together, continuing in the Apostles' doctrine and Fellowship, in the breaking of Bread, and the Prayers; all in perfect unity of feeling, in singleness of heart serving God; no man saying that aught of the things which he possessed were his own, but parting them to every man, according as he had need, and so having all things common? This was not Communism, as some have supposed. Each man's property was his own. His bestowal of it was entirely voluntary. What S. Peter said to Ananias, who had pretended to give all, but retained a part, and in such pretense lying to the Holy Ghost: "Whilst it remained, was it not thine own, and after it was sold, was it not in thine own power?" proves clearly enough that personal ownership was not discarded. The same is evident from the whole narrative of the wonderful charity and generous giving of those Apostolic Christians in the first days of the Church, who sold all their possessions and goods, and placed the whole price of the things sold at the disposal of the Apostles. Love of Christ, love of the brethren, was simply acting itself out in entire unselfishness. They were voluntarily making the best use possible, each as his judgment so influenced, impelled him, of the means God had intrusted to his stewardship. Christian society ought to come, at all times, as near to this grand ideal as possible. It was then for a brief time fully realized, as S. Paul everywhere insists, that all in the Church are "members of Christ, and every one members one of another."

The Church, indeed, is in its very nature a social institution. No man can stand apart from his brother. Whatever there may be in this world to estrange and divide, here there must be a oneness of love and sympathy, of sentiment and belief, of desire, purpose and endeavor. The ties that bind all in one are the most real and strong that can be conceived. This unity and fellowship must be practically attained or the Church cannot fulfil her mission in bringing home the Gospel of temporal as well as spiritual salvation to the great masses of mankind. Our own observation will readily teach us that if the Church does not provide for the social wants of the people, they will seek such provision elsewhere. Man is a social being. He is made for society. He cannot live in isolation. He must have fellowship with others. Persons of like tastes are necessarily drawn together. They find in one another that enjoyment so necessary to all and without which life would be intolerable.

There are many forms of association not evil in themselves, but for the most part needless, had the Church done her duty to the people to whom she is sent. The Masonic fraternity presupposes the Old Testament, and its recognition of the Christian Calendar, the principles of Christian morals, and the theologic virtues, shows that it reverences the New. Indeed, the whole Bible is avowedly its greatest light. Odd Fellowship is like Masonry healthful in its influence and beneficent in character. Christian men often feel themselves justified in seeking in one or other of these societies that companionship and social enjoyment which the Christian society has failed to provide. Possibly some who are indifferent or hostile to Christianity encourage themselves in remaining outside the Church, on the ground that such societies, contrary to their intention, do for them all that the Church could do for her members. Many other secret societies have come into existence within the last few years, each having some worthy or philanthropic object, and all alike offering, to workingmen especially, some of the social advantages which they crave. The cost of membership is large, especially when the same men, as is usually the case, belong to several of them. Large demands are made upon the time and labor of their adherents. They serve, among other purposes, on week-day evenings, to provide pleasant companionship and association. One can scarcely regret this when outside the lodge there are generally no pleasant, well-warmed and lighted rooms in which to pass an evening except the bar-room, the saloon or the dance halls, in all our frontier towns. The small, cold bedroom in the boarding-house is too uncomfortable. What

are men to do who have no homes? The Church does
nothing for them. Society does not regard them. It is no
wonder that such fraternities grow and multiply, and that
the real wants they in great measure supply, and the dues
necessary to sustain them are in the way of the Church
reclaiming her rightful place and influence among the
people.

The late Bishop of Manchester is credited with a saying, as true as it is wise: "It is not so important to
Christianize Socialism as to socialize Christianity." This
is the problem before us now: how to socialize Christianity? Solve this problem, and all others which so
alarm the patriot and the Christian will soon find their
solution. Real Christianity, effectively brought to the
hearts and minds of the people, in all its power and beneficence, is the sure remedy for the evils which we dread,
and which must find a remedy, or the prophets of evil
cannot well exaggerate them.

The Church has abundantly proved her ability to meet
the social as well as other needs of all sorts and conditions
of men. This was pre-eminently the case in Apostolic and
primitive times. In the Ancient Church every baptized
person was supposed really to have renounced the world
for the service of Christ and the brethren. There was, up
to the early part of the fourth century, a complete separa-
tion between Christian and worldly society. Christians
found in the society of one another, in their social wor-

ship, in their common hopes, common associations and common plans of Christian effort, the satisfaction of all social wants. The well-being of one was the well-being of all. They who were God's stewards in the possession of wealth, held all their means subject to the needs of the community. None could be in want, none could be left to suffer, when all were ready with generous aid and sympathy to minister relief. The charity of the primitive Church is the wonder of later ages. All in the Church were brethren. They loved one another, with a pure heart, fervently. Their mutual affection was so marked as to excite the admiration even of the heathen. "See how these Christians love one another!" was their frequent exclamation.

The Church, in our times, has lost much of this whole-souled communion of all classes. Protestantism rejected all the forms of Monasticism, all the Orders in which the desire for the realization of Christian brotherhood had found expression in evil days, but put nothing in their place. So far as the Church has failed to retain her hold upon the common people, it has been mainly because she has not adequately responded to their social requirements. Some denominations have sought to supply this defect in our modern Christianity, in modes which, though not always successful, have yet served to give them popularity. The prayer meeting, class meeting, conference meeting, have a strong socializing influence. These and like instrumentalities are not evil in themselves.   They may be good. The danger is in their abuse, in their giving scope to obvious faults of human nature.   They could only win approval among Churchmen if kept clear of extravagances, and if so conducted as not to promote fanaticism, the Pharisaic spirit of self-conceit and the humiliation of the diffident and humble-minded.

Besides the socializing effect of public worship, which cannot be what it is intended to be and naturally would be in this regard, unless all are brought into relations of acquaintance and mutual interest and sympathy, there is scarcely any provision in the Church for combining all classes of the people socially on a religious basis.   The various guilds and societies which are found in different parishes, sewing societies, mite societies, sociables and the like, seldom answer the purpose here in view, whatever good in other respects they may accomplish.   In the organizing of missions or new parishes there is much combination to secure temporal prosperity, and often for true spiritual growth.   All are drawn closely together by common plans of work.   Every stranger is at once visited, introduced, and made to feel at home.   All whose interest can be secured receive due attention.   Seats and Prayer Books are provided for all who come to the place of worship.   No effort is spared to gain their attachment and secure their help in the common work.   Class distinctions are scarcely perceptible.   Societies are formed for various purposes. All join them and co-operate for their success. The unity and cordial co-operation of all is irresistibly attractive to many who are without.

If the spirit that pervades such new organizations could be made continuous and constant, the Church would make wonderful progress. She would do much to win the masses of the people to her allegiance. But as parishes increase in numbers and become pecuniarily strong, as populations become dense and Church buildings large, the methods which have proved financially, and in their social and religious influence, so successful, are discontinued. Many who come to Church are entirely unacquainted. They are not looked after and visited unless they are people of position. The poor straying into the Church are too generally unrecognized. Members of the same congregation have no interest in one another. After years of common worship they remain strangers. The non-Church-going classes are not sought out, and invited and shown by practical proofs of interest in their welfare that they would find in the Church a welcome and a spiritual home.

Why should this be so? Why could not all, through the long years of the life of every parish, be bound together in the same close bonds of fellowship? But we know too well that this is not the case, and the result is everywhere disastrous.

In every good class in the Sunday-school there is a

strong social feeling. The class is a little Christian society
Mutual acquaintance ensures interest in one another.
They strive to keep up the good character of the class for
contributions, scholarship and good behavior. Their fellowship leads to strong friendships, often lasting through
life. The like results should be found in the Sunday-
school as a whole. It is promoted by common worship
and instruction; by frequent meetings for practice in singing; by catechizing and recitations, and by the great
Christian Festivals and their proper observance. Picnics
and excursions, if properly conducted, are useful expe-
dients. At all events, they are eminently socializing.

But when boys leave the Sunday-school, which is generally too soon—when their only connection with religious
institutions is to be maintained by attendance at Church,
they sadly miss that element which had retained and
made them happy in the Sunday-school. The Church is
to them formal, unsocial. Its atmosphere is to them
cold; repellent rather than attractive. Scarcely any one
seems to be interested in them ; there is nothing to draw
them except duty. Though they had once learned to love
the services, their social instincts are not satisfied. They
seek their companions out of the Church. They learn to
frequent places of vulgar amusement. Vice, seen often in
those with whom they associate, loses its hideousness.
Their companionships are found in forbidden places of
resort. It is a marvel if they do not learn to practice the

vices of those about them. Indifference leads to infidelity. Thriftlessness, profanity, intemperance, licentiousness, come of evil associations, and entail hopeless ruin of body and soul.

There is great fault, no doubt, in families. Every home should be made attractive. The little home circle should be made so pleasant, so genial, so full of affection, so abounding in social gratifications, that there could be no temptation strong enough to draw the virtuous young man strong in Christian principles, into dangerous associations. But it is to be feared such homes are very few, even among professing Christians. Rarely, indeed, do we find them among those not yet Christianized, in the middle and lower classes. Still more rarely, perhaps, in unchristianized families of the wealthy.

As so many homes are unworthy of the name, and the Church does not do her duty in satisfying the social wants of the people, not only are boys led to resorts for pleasure that are not always free from vice, but men of all ages and classes consort together for the social excitements of drinking, and playing, and gambling. One of the modern institutions for social purposes among the socially respectable, is the Club. I would not altogether condemn it. I would like to see here a Church Club, like those already in operation in some cities. The Club meets a demand not otherwise provided for. It may be purely literary. It may be for innocent and healthful amusements. It may subserve the cultivation of good fellowship. But it may degenerate. The secular social club may, under influences not likely to be excluded, be characterized by drinking, playing, and other social sins. The Church club, or the workingman's club under Church auspices, would not be liable to these abuses.

That husband and father has but a poor idea of his duty to his family who leaves them habitually to seek his society elsewhere. Let him spend his evenings at home. Let him do his part to make his home so delightful that he will feel no need to go from it for genial companionship. How large an increase of happiness might he not thus secure, to himself and to those who should be nearest and dearest to him !

One of the first duties of the Church is to make pleasant Christian homes among the working classes. Let those Christian women of social position, intelligence and refinement, who have made their own homes what they ought to be, seek to extend their influence for the forming of others on the same model. Let them put off all conventionality of manners. Let them learn that outward station does not necessarily make character. Let them seek and find sterling qualities in all, independently of outward surroundings. Let them learn to go among the humble and poor, without patronizing airs, which would nullify all their influence for good. Let them make frequent and regular visitations at the homes of the poor, and of those who depend for support upon their daily labor. Let them win the confidence of these, by manifest solicitude for their good. Having done this, let them patiently try to elevate them to their own standard of Christian feeling. Let them give kindly instruction in household duties, in the virtues of tidiness, economy and thrift, in family government, in the ways of making their homes pleasant to husbands and children. This is the way to spread Christianity, and to win the people to Christ and the Church. We have seen grand success crowning such efforts. They must succeed, if the perseverance and wisdom with which they are attempted are equal to the discouragements to be overcome.

The object, then, to be had in view in every parish, should be to bring about a social feeling between all the people of the Church, and especially between those who constitute "society," so-called, and those whose life is one of manual toil. By socializing Christianity we are to make the Church the power of God it was intended to be among the masses of mankind.

To make the Church the social force contemplated, various modes are used by those who would carry on Christ's work in His spirit, and who see the necessity of real brotherhood among divers classes, in order to effective, aggressive work among them. Among these may be mentioned: Sewing or industrial schools for girls; girls Friendly societies; mothers' meetings for women; St.

Andrew's Brotherhoods, or like organizations for young men; Bible classes for men; cottage lectures for working people; reading-rooms and workingmen's clubs, in connection with the Church, and fostered by Church people.

"Where there is a will, there is a way." You who give serious and prayerful consideration to the work to be done, will readily find means and modes of doing it. The wisest planning, the most perfect details of an organization will never of themselves accomplish the results. Rise to something like an adequate conception of what needs to be done. Consider it till you adequately feel its importance and necessity. Then undertake it with prayer and reliance on the Divine blessing.

Plans of organization are only useful as supplying instructive hints, and showing the results of experience. You can find in the Church periodicals sufficient information in regard to the starting and carrying on of any of these instrumentalities. The Pastor who has decided upon any one of them has but to inform himself thoroughly about it, find the suitable place for its meetings, and then select and instruct his agents. It is of little use to give notice from the Church that he wants helpers. They will not generally volunteer. We must assume, if we really believe in the Church and her work of evangelization, that there are fit persons for any work she is called to do, and that all her members must have some part in it. It is the function of the Pastor to call upon the workers and distribute the work among them. The difficulties are not to be disguised. But Church people will do Church work, if shown how. They must be individually asked, and urged, encouraged and instructed. They cannot but respond to the urgency of the call, when perseveringly, lovingly presented. For responsible positions, let those be selected who are most competent, for piety, intelligent love of the Church, and good social position. Teach them their duties. Place upon them and hold them to their responsibility, then trust them. Give them wide discretion as you find them worthy of it, not interfering in petty details, nor seeming to take their work out of their hands. They will generally reward your confidence.

In a parish in a poor but populous neighborhood, a woman of tact, practical good sense, earnest devotion, love of girls and power to win their love, starts a sewing-school. She first canvasses the whole district. She secures the attendance of half a dozen girls. She provides materials for needle-work, for making up plain garments. The girls are interested. The short prayers, the spirited hymns, the familiar talks, the work assigned, are thoroughly enjoyed. One, two or more assistants are employed. The visiting is kept up and extended. The school grows. The interest increases. In a few months, on every Saturday afternoon the place is full. They are beginning to come to the Sunday-school. Here they are welcomed by their teachers, who have made them friends. The mothers cannot but appreciate what is done, and the unselfish interest taken. The fathers are not unaffected. I need not picture the change for the better soon observable in the tone and manners of the scholars and in the home life of the families reached by the blessed influences coming to pervade the district. The congregations increase. The socializing influence from such a simple agency is telling wonderfully in the building up of the parish.

The weekly mothers' meeting may soon follow. Secure the room in connection with the Church, if possible— every parish that is able ought to have a Parish House for Church work and social purposes—though this is not absolutely essential. Find a competent lady who will give herself heart and soul to the work. Her own heart full of the work, she will inspire others and find assistants. Incessant visiting will by and by bring in a few women. Let work be provided, the materials furnished at cost. Teach the processes of cutting, fitting, as necessary. They may work for their own families. They may help to supply clothing for the destitute. They may earn something for missions. Cultivate their self-respect and self-dependence. Let useful conversation, adapted to teach, enliven their work, and read occasionally something interesting and with a profitable lesson. The labors over, the Bible lesson is read, and there is singing and prayer. Books are lent to those who will read. Church papers are supplied. A real affectionate interest is taken in the temporal concerns of all who are visited, and represented in the meetings. In large parishes there is usually more than one district where mothers' meetings may be organized. Such work once begun will grow. One method of socializing and reaching the people will suggest the need of others. The fathers interested through their children and wives will be brought into Bible classes. The workingman's club, the free reading-room, the St. Andrew's Brotherhood, will come as the demand for them is felt. One of the greatest advantages of free seats in Church is that all may find a welcome and a home in the House of God.

It will serve a good purpose to have an occasional evening meeting for refreshments and social intercourse, at which all the families, fathers, mothers and children, even to the youngest of those reached by such works of love, shall be present. They will be served by the Rector and others, gentlemen and ladies prominent in the parish, committees for various subdivisions of the work. Short addresses will be made. The Bishop, if he can be present, will add his congratulations. Thus you would have a social gathering, such as Christ enjoined upon those who would make a feast, which would give joy to His heart and cause rejoicing in Heaven.

I need not go into further detail. It is sufficient to suggest how the older girls in the Sunday-school, employed in shops, and stores, and offices, may be brought into social relations under Christian ladies, who would strengthen their moral and religious principles, and protect them at a time of life and in the midst of surroundings full of the greatest perils ; how boys of various ages may be organized socially for healthful amusements, and secular combined with religious instruction, under Church influence ; how all classes may, through fit agencies, be brought into social relations, the end and outcome of which shall be membership in the Divine Society of the Church of God, and the blessedness of its communion.

In small places, most of the special forms of work here suggested are inapplicable. Common sense must judge what is most likely to succeed. Because in large towns or cities an elaborate machinery with many branches of work is successful, it does not follow that the same thing is to be everywhere attempted. The plans must be suited to the special field. But in all parishes and missions, even the smallest, something may and should be done, though it be but by a guild for girls or women, or a boys' or men's society, to bring to bear a social influence, to help those who are within the Church, and to win others and increase the membership, and build up Christ's Kingdom in the community.

Are not such works worth attempting? To those who shall thus seek to fulfil their "vocation and ministry" as Christians, shall there not be a great reward? Shall they not win an approving conscience and the smile of Heaven, and the glorious reward of those who turn many to right- eousness? Let us begin thus to fulfil our bounden duties, and go on, as God shall lead and guide us.

VII.

ON LAY HELP IN EXTENDING PASTORAL CARE OVER ALL WHO CAN BE BROUGHT INTO THE CHURCH.

Genesis iv, 9: Am I my brother's keeper?

THIS was the question that was asked by Cain when God called him to account for the disappearance of his brother Abel. He asked it as if the answer must be negative. It was the first suggestion of his sinful heart to deny that he was his brother's keeper. The Cains of this world have ever since, under like circumstances, reiterated the same question. We should scarcely suppose it would be asked by persons of a different class, or that any would deny that we all have a certain responsibility in regard to our brethren. But strange as it would appear, there are professing Christians who ask it with the same incredulous implication when the duty is pressed home upon them of caring for all sorts and conditions of men.

In a most true sense we are our brother's keeper. All men do in their hearts accept the teaching of the parable of the good Samaritan. Not in the Church, not even in the world, can the theory be acted on that each may live and care only for himself. There must be mutual sympathy and offices of love between those who come in contact with each other, or the Church would be a nullity and human intercourse impossible. Especially must Christians recognize the universally accepted fact and truth of the common brotherhood of man. They especially whom Providence has favored with the gifts of intelligence, wealth, or social position, must lend the helping hand of brotherly sympathy and kindly service to those who in any respect, by the disposals of the same Providence, have been less fortunate. The Parish or Mission is organized for mutual care and helpfulness among all whom its agencies shall bring into the fold of Christ. It is of primary importance that a pastoral care should be extended over every member. What are some of the modes in which Christians who own that they *are* their brother's keeper, can render their assistance in this work? The enquiry is necessary, if we would learn how best to work our Parishes.

The Church is God's family. All baptized persons are members of Christ, the children of God, and inheritors of the Kingdom of Heaven. We all know how necessary it is that parents should exercise the most watchful supervision over their children. Parents are rightly held responsible for such training and care of their offspring as shall guard them against dissoluteness, and prepare and strengthen them to meet the temptations and trials of their growing years. In the present condition of the

world it is quite as necessary that there should be constant, watchful care on the part of Pastors and people
over every member of the family of Christ.

Consider the various classes of people to whom such
pastoral care is indispensable, if they are to be kept safely
within the fold and nourished unto eternal life.

It is fearful to contemplate the number of communicants who relapse into the world, and still more fearful to
reflect upon the reason, that they were not sufficiently
watched over and tended when once the vows of God were
upon them of their voluntary choice.

Pastoral oversight is exceedingly important when the
congregation is composed of intelligent people whose surroundings are favorable to religion. Circumstances are
constantly arising when they individually need the
Pastor's personal counsel and that of Christians of matured
wisdom and experience. The loving Pastor should be
ever at hand, so that all in trouble, doubt or any spiritual
difficulty may open their griefs to his confiding ear and
receive advice, encouragement and consolation. So, too,
Christians should bear one another's burdens and thus
fulfil the law of Christ.

But when we consider the young, those of both sexes
verging upon manhood and womanhood, the poor,
the immature, the ignorant and those in untoward conditions of life, the need of pastoral oversight and friendly,
sympathizing, thoughtful care and counsel are greatly

increased. If the Church is awake to the necessity of meeting the wants of such as these, how painful must be the consciousness of past neglect, how fervent the prayer for greater faithfulness in pastoral duty !

If so many communicants are yearly left to fall away, how much greater the number of baptized persons who never become living Christians, or who, at least since their childhood, have been wholly of the world. From defective family training and associations, unfaithful sponsors, evil companionship and godless surroundings, they lose all connection with those who are constituted their spiritual guides, and fall into habits of worldliness and impenitence. In the order of spiritual causes, every baptized person, being in the state of grace and salvation, ought to grow up in faith and obedience and the saving knowledge of Jesus Christ, to be pillars of strength and beauty in the Church. Yet many, may it not be said the majority, of those brought within the Christian Covenant, are living as if they were without, practically aliens from the Spiritual Israel, without the Christian hope, without God in the world ! What a fearful responsibility rests upon Pastors and Christian people for these redeemed and lost souls ! Surely it is worth our best thought and efforts to remedy a state of things so appalling.

Again, we are receiving constantly a large influx of population, of whom many belong by baptism and early education to the Church in England, Ireland, Scotland,

and in the Eastern States. They are largely of the laboring classes. They leave their native country and their
homes for the higher wages and the more equal social conditions of this "land of freedom," or for the fancied opportunities of making or bettering their fortunes in the
wild frontier towns of the West. Many of them leave
their Church and their religion behind them. We often
hear people in and beyond the mountains in Colorado, who
have failed in their ventures, talking about "going back to
God's country." In these high altitudes, with the stupendous wonders of nature about them, they should feel
themselves nearer to God and Heaven, and their righteousness should "stand like the strong mountains." But the
nearer God may be to them in nature, the farther they are
from God revealed in His Word and in His Church. In
this land of their adoption the Church seldom seeks them
out. If there be a Church accessible, they do not find it.
Their garb seems more becoming to very different associations. Without friends in the Church, all connected with
it being strangers, with no friendships to draw them, no
ties to bind them to it, except duty; faring hard, perhaps,
in their struggle of life for themselves and their families,
they are indisposed to seek its spiritual privileges and
comfort. Their infidelity to the Church under the circumstances is but natural, and to be expected. Even in
the exceptional instances, when they are sought out by
some kind-hearted Pastor and by sympathizing Christians,

and brought home to the old Church of their early love, and their hearts warmed, and for the time responding to Christian truth, prompting the realization of their Christian obligations; soon compelled by the exigencies of their hard life to remove to some other locality, they again relapse into neglect and indifference. There are, thank God, many exceptions even among those least favored by fortune, but abundant facts justify our general statement.

It is scarcely different with the poorer classes of our home population. If they are once brought effectively under the influence of the Church, their frequent removals soon carry them beyond its reach. Apart from the Church's care and the means of grace, there is no power to hold men to Christianity. To attempt to live an inward Christian life without open profession and connection with the Church's corporate and sacramental life, must result in failure. The Christianity of those who are not in the visible organic living Body of Christ, soon becomes invisible, imperceptible and powerless over the life and character.

It is easy to say of all the baptized of every class that they ought to adhere to the Church wherever they are, and under all circumstances, and so to maintain their Christian integrity. But is this to be expected? And is the fault wholly on their side? Should not the Church be what Christ was, the shepherd of her people? Should she not gather them into the fold and tend and feed them as the one flock of Christ? Should she not go out into the wilderness, or wherever they are straying, and seek them in whatever perilous places, and take them to her arms and bear them upon her shoulders, and gently bring them back to her safe enclosure, where they shall have plenty, and peace, and rest? Should not these be her *special* care, because of their greater needs? Will it not be more to her praise and an occasion of greater rejoicing to bring home the wanderers, than merely to keep those who are already safely sheltered? We ought to know well how our Lord would answer such questions as these.

No communicant should ever remove permanently to another place without taking a letter of commendation from his Pastor to the Rector or Missionary in charge at or nearest to his new residence, and presenting it at once on his arrival. The law of the Church requires this. If not asked for, it should still always be given. If this law were observed in all cases, we should have less cause to deplore our losses.

The importance of heeding this requirement of regular transfer and acceptance of Church members, cannot be too strongly urged. It is so easy to postpone religious duties, to break away from the ties of the Church, to neglect Church attendance and sacramental privileges in a new place, under new associations. Every means should be used to prevent it. A letter of commendation is a testimonial. It guarantees the Christian character of the bearer. It is the best possible introduction. It wins immediate confidence. It procures admission into Christian society. It gives position and secures opportunities of Christian usefulness.

But it involves reciprocal duties on the part of those who are to receive and welcome the strangers thus accredited. They should immediately call upon them and with open arms adopt them into their fellowship. They should show themselves so friendly and cordial to strangers as to remove all possibility of their feeling that they are in an atmosphere of coldness and neglect. How much room there is for improvement in this regard! Is it not the fact that many a stranger accredited or known to some of us as belonging to the Church, is with us for months without receiving the slightest Christian recognition?

Our duty is the same, whether strangers coming among us bring a letter of transfer or not. We are to show them Christian politeness. We are to give them Christian hospitality. We are so to demean ourselves that they shall feel that they have not left the Church behind in their old home. It is with them still. The same service of prayer and praise invites their worship. The same God and Saviour waits to answer and bless them. The same pulpit instructions afford them the means of increase of knowledge, and counsel and admonition. The same Holy Table offers them, if worthily prepared, the Bread from

Heaven, the Flesh and Blood of Christ, to nourish their souls and bodies unto everlasting life. They may still feel that they are one in the catholic communion of the Saints. To the old friendships new ones are added. Thus all the embarrassments, all the unfavorable conditions of their new sphere are to be compensated.

To meet all these requisitions for pastoral oversight of all these classes of people, in this land and this age of worldly engrossments, is surely of the greatest importance. The communicants, the baptized and unconfirmed, children and youths, the poor, the toiling masses of the people, strangers of every condition, must be visited, cared for, shown the most loving sympathy and interest, kept within the fold, or if wandering away, brought back, helped in every way, as Christ aided all with whom He came in contact, by bearing their infirmities, to lead them to the Source of Healing for their sins.

The greatest responsibility rests upon Pastors. They are to have something of the pastoral heart that was in Christ. They are to be good under-shepherds. They are to know and call each one by name, and lead them together and individually into the green pastures and beside the still waters of refreshment. They are to seek the lost till found. If the work required by the Canons of the Church, of keeping accurate lists of families, baptized persons, the confirmed, the communicants—in order to an individual acquaintance and influence over each and all, and that he may often, as he looks through his list of people, pray for each one—be of great difficulty in large towns, and among shifting populations, nevertheless, it should be done, even though other and less important duties be neglected. How can one be a true Pastor to people *in the mass?* The pastoral relation is with individuals. It is a heart to heart relation. The power of the Ministry is not in pulpit oratory, not in learned discourse to congregations; it is in house to house and heart to heart teaching. It is in personal influence. It is in preaching Christ by word and example, in His mercy and beneficence to soul and body, by going about healing all manner of diseases and infirmities among the people.

But the Pastor can not do all this alone. His office as Pastor is not exclusive. If he is to have no help in the work of pastoral oversight and care of his flock, all that is demanded of the Church in our times can not be done. She must confess her inability to apply the Gospel effectively to all classes and conditions of men. She must yield her claim to actual catholicity. She must be a class church, a sect among sects, a mere denomination. For it is utterly impossible for the clergyman, without assistance from his people, to afford that care and attention in sickness and in health, and under all the varying circumstances and conditions of life, that is indispensable to permanent benefit to all rightfully belonging to his cure and for whom he is responsible. He must invoke lay co-operation in this as in all his work. The success of a Pastor is largely determined by his ability to interest and gather around him workers, to call out and develop their several capabilities, and to gain their confidence in his judgment in directing them what to do and how best to do it. The people must respond to his appeals for help. If they do not co-operate with the Minister they are counteracting his influence. The more indifferent they are, the harder they make his labors. Our Lord's saying is as true here as anywhere: "he that is not with Me is against Me." The Minister must have the earnest prayers, the hearty sympathy, the active, zealous co-operation of his people, or great success is not to be expected. His lay workers should, as far as possible, be organized. Their work should be on a plan. Their combined efforts should be directed to the bringing of the people who are without, of all ages and conditions, into the Church, and holding them with cords of love, that they may be built up and edified in Christ and be living stones in the spiritual temple of Christianity.

In initiating such work the following hints may be useful: The Pastor, knowing intimately all his people, has upon his hands some who are ill, some bed-ridden persons, some very poor and wretched, some suffering in bereavement and some in loss of property, or other misfortune. He will know the fit persons to go and minister to all these according to their needs, to read to them, to pray with them, sympathize with them, to sit with them, in silence and tears sharing their sorrows, or to take to them little delicacies and tokens of love and sympathy. Here is a street whose denizens are unknown. And here are two women who are bidden to visit every house and tenement and report their condition in temporal and spiritual things. Some children will be found for the Sunday-school; some members for the congregation; some in affliction who need and will be brought to receive the consolations of the Gospel. There is a family or a sick man or woman to whom daily or weekly visits will bring comfort; and there is a good woman who shall make such visits, with readings and prayers, and kind words and acts of sympathy. Here in the suburbs of the place, or near a manufactory is a neighborhood that ought to be visited. It will not do to take it for granted that all who live there are Roman Catholics or Methodists, or of any or all of the denominations. There may be Church people there. There may be recruits for the Sunday-school. It may be found that a Mission school, or a sewing-school, or a mothers' meeting, or a cottage lecture, should be established. And here are two or three young men of good sense and Christian purpose, and here are two or three women, qualified in like manner, who may be appointed and induced to look carefully through the whole district, and by house to house visitation find out and report just who and what all the people are who inhabit it. There will always be some outcome to such work. Some good results will follow. It will be found necessary that the visits be continued. They will bring to many a wholesome and a religious influence. They will bring to some the Gospel of Christ with all its priceless blessings.

As was said in a former lecture, the Christian layman can often reach laymen who shun the clergyman—whom the clergyman cannot approach. The Pastor cannot get so near many of the men of his charge as to know intimately their thoughts and feelings, what they converse about, what their attitude towards spiritual things. The godly layman may mingle among them, win their esteem, confidence and friendship, draw them out, get at the secrets of their hearts, so far as they have any, in relation to God, to Christianity and the Church of Christ, and thus gain a position in which to have great influence for good to their souls. The clergyman is thought to be an official, to do what his office requires, to speak perfunctorily, and not to understand the men who are not of his own class, or who move in other spheres. This estimate is altogether wrong concerning most of the clergy. But it tends to hinder or weaken their influence. They ought to go down among the people, and learn to sympathize with them in all their labors and trials, and speak to them in their own language. Yet however near they may get to them, they must have helpers in their work to make their work effective. Their laymen must learn, under their training, to be missionaries, preachers, evangelists, visitors, under or assist-ant pastors. Surely this Church of ours, bringing into effect all her latent forces in her lay membership, might win back the many who are alienated from Christianity and make herself as catholic in practice as she is in theory and of right. May God hasten the time.

We might learn many a valuable lesson from those bodies of Christians in this country who seem most thoroughly to have won the confidence of the working classes. The Roman Catholics and the Methodists do not undervalue the prerogatives of their clergy, while they call forth to the fullest extent the co-operation of their laity. You will find the devoted Sisters of Charity wherever there is suffering: in the hospital, the tent, the prisoner's cell, the lonely garret, the crowded, filthy tene-ments of the poor. You will find them soliciting con-tributions in remote hamlets, and mining camps, among men whose exterior appearance must cause heart-sinking and fear; schooling themselves to courage and boldness in their cause, and thus gaining the means to build and support great institutions of charity: wholly self-forgetful, anxious only to do good, angels of mercy to the sick and dying, more helpful to strengthen their church in strong foundations of beneficence, than all the wealth of the rich—an arm of power the greatness of which is beyond human estimate. You will find brotherhoods of men and sisterhoods of women giving their lives to teaching and controlling religious education far beyond their own communion. You will find lay organizations of every sort and for every purpose adapted to hold the people to the faith and order of the Church.

So, too, among our Methodist brethren. It is well to study their practical system, and learn what is the secret of its effectiveness. We shall doubtless find some things that we must account as evils both in Romanism and Methodism, that make for popularity. As in the former, the easiness with which peace of conscience may be gained, and the weakening of the sense of responsibility in belief and conduct, so in the latter, the excess of emotionalism, the confounding of regeneration with conversion, and of conversion with personal assurance of acceptance with God and a sense of sinless perfection, like the doctrine of the indefectibility of Grace in another school, may lead to antinomianism, and the practical denial that sin is sin in the believer. These things do unquestionably tend to win large favor and acceptance with many people who are not theologically well informed. But there is much to approve in Methodism, much retained from the Anglican Church that belongs to the very life of Christianity; much that it is our duty to hold and practice, that we are too apt to leave in abeyance, and that gives the system a hold upon religious minds, especially of the middle and working classes. The founders of the system were Churchmen, who were resolved to the last never to leave the Church. It was the leaders in the Church in a cold and barren age who knew not how to approve and encourage what was good in them, and thus prevent a schism. We do not want their sensationalism. But we do want their warm-heartedness, their zeal in lay instruction and the conversion of souls, their devotion to good works, their watchful care of their members, their *esprit du corps*, and unity and co-operation in everything that can help to prosper and extend their cause. God grant that the time may soon come when they shall acknowledge the sin and evils of schism, and the inefficacy for permanent good of human arrangements so far as substituted for the Apostolic and Divine, and return to the Body they confessed to be Christ's, and left with reluctance, bringing with them their warm and earnest life to vivify the Body and be its ornament and glory.

Let us learn to imitate them in the good they do, and in so far as they imitate the Saviour. Our own people will not then fall into their ranks for the sake of the confidence and sympathy they find among them. We shall gain more fully than they have done and be able to bless with far greater and more enduring spiritual benefits the common people; and Christ's intention will be fulfilled in the new proof of the divinity of His religion, that "the Gospel is preached to the poor."

Our Church is fast gaining the realization of her catho-

lic heritage.   We have already our sisterhoods and orders
of deaconesses, without objectionable features and abuses.
We have our Church schools of acknowledged superiority
in the completeness of their secular and religious training,
so that there is no shadow of excuse for those who would
place their children under training that would by insen-
sible degrees educate out of them their Church principles
and pervert them from their faith.   We have our hospitals
and other like institutions of charity in the Church for
the care and relief of God's poor and afflicted ones, and for
conferring the blessings the Saviour came to bestow upon
the bodies as well as the souls of men.   These works are
growing among us.   They bring honor and strength to
the Church.   They are helping her influence with the
people. By ministering to men's sicknesses and infirmities,
as did our blessed Lord, we get access for the Church to
the hearts of men.   So the love of Christ brings to all salvation.   In all these works the ministry of the brethren to
individuals is secured and gives success.

The principle contended for is generally acknowledged.
Sunday-school teachers are expected to visit their scholars
regularly at their homes, to care for them in sickness, to
enlist the interest of their parents in the services of the
Church.   So also the instructors of Bible classes, those
who are at the head of guilds and industrial schools, or
who conduct cottage lectures.   We must carry out the
principle fully.   All must be led to feel that it is part of

their " vocation and ministry " as Christians, to show the proofs of their love and obedience to Christ by doing all the good they are able to individual souls, and thus aid in the pastoral work of the Ministry.

God grant to us all new zeal in His service. God bless to us the improvement of our advantages for gathering in, sheltering, feeding, nourishing in the fold of Christ the poor sinners who are perishing for lack of the knowledge of the Gospel of the kingdom of Christ, which it is our work to give to them. God grant that with the life of Christ in our heart, following in His blessed footsteps, in the lanes and alleys, and byways and highways, in the haunts of publicans and sinners, wherever there are souls feeding on husks and starving for the Bread of Life, or imperfect Christians needing to be nourished to the full stature of Christian manhood, WE MAY GO ABOUT DOING GOOD.

As Mothers' Meetings have been recommended in the foregoing lectures, there is here appended from a " Manual of Mothers' Meetings," published by the author in 1871, now out of print, the following

DIRECTIONS FOR MOTHERS' MEETINGS.

1. In a large, compactly built city, it may be best to have one central Mothers' meeting connected with each Parish

or Mission, under the charge of a lady with her assistants. But there are generally in and about a small city or large village, separate neighborhoods, growing up in consequence of manufactories or other local interests, being in some cases quite distant from each other and from the Parish Church or Churches, each having a community feeling of its own. In each of these districts, Cottage lectures and Mothers' meetings should be established, as a means of winning the people to the Church, adding to the strength of the Parish and opening the way, with God's blessing, to new Missions and Parishes. In the territory embraced in St. Paul's Parish, there are five or six such districts. Most of the Mission stations in our home field would be greatly strengthened by the use of one or both these instrumentalities. Sewing or industrial schools for girls and night schools may also be added with the best results.

2. The lady appointed to take charge of a Mothers' meeting may begin by visiting to bring people to the Cottage lectures. Let her also, if able to do so, increase her practical knowledge by visiting an efficient Mothers' meeting already in operation. She should embrace every opportunity made for her by the Minister, or which she can find for herself under his sanction, to visit, read to and pray with habitually some sick person or persons, and thus learn to aim directly to bring the Gospel home to them, to convert them and help them to grow in grace. Such methods of gaining knowledge and experience will be effectual in every Parish if faithfully used; and it is to be hoped that opportunities will be afforded ere long to perfect the instruction thus obtained, in training-houses for parochial work in this and in many other dioceses, in connection with Church Homes, Hospitals and Sisterhoods.

3. Having become familiar with the district and acquainted with the women to be most relied on, let the meeting be appointed at some convenient private house, and visit thoroughly, inviting attendance. The meeting may be held weekly at different houses according to convenience, or regularly in the mission school, if the Church has one in the district

4. The service to be as hereinafter [in the Manual referred to] appointed. If the conductor of the meeting does not sing, an assistant should be secured who can. That which is read should be furnished or approved by the Rector. Any exposition of Scripture, if attempted, should not be doctrinal, but entirely practical. Children and even babies may be present and work may go on, *e. g.*, sewing, being only suspended for the worship, in which all should be taught to join with intelligence and heartiness. Sometimes it may be desirable that all should work in common for some charitable or missionary object.

5. The aim should be to cultivate personal religion in the members, their husbands and all connected with them ; to bring them to the open confession of Christ, regular attendance at Church and the Holy Communion, and earnestness in all religious duties ; to make their homes attractive ; to encourage and help the Christian training of their children, and to promote thrift and industry, and mutual love and helpfulness. All should have Bibles, Prayer Books and Hymnals, and be taught how to use them. The Rector should often attend, and when present will, of course, conduct the devotions and teaching. He will thus be able to give much encouragement and assistance. Coming in near the close, he may give a five minutes' practical sermon or instruction.

6. Visits should be frequent to all within the district who will receive them, and especially to those who are sick or in affliction, not neglecting to propose reading and prayer before leaving, if there be opportunity and it can be done unobtrusively.

The visitors will be at no loss for topics of conversation, even when strangers are called upon, if it be remembered that the first object is to awaken interest and win confidence by showing real interest in them, in their children, and in their pursuits, and to ascertain their spiritual condition and religious habits ; to remove hindrances to their attendance at Church and taking their children to Church and Sunday-school ; to bring them under personal instruction and the social influence of the best who attend the meeting, and to help them to self-consecration to Christ, and a life of faith and prayer.

7.　Those who conduct the meetings should point out the ways in which the women can do good for Christ's sake : such as taking care of the sick; "minding" a child for a little while; helping a feeble neighbor wash, or do some household work; and such other little offices of kindness as a Christian's common sense will readily suggest.

8.　Let the conductor of the meeting lose no opportunity to win the affections of the women, not only by visiting in sickness, but by carrying to them, when they are sick, hospital stores and taking books or playthings to amuse their children when they are ill; by helping those who are poor to help themselves, rather than giving them too much and thus creating a dependent spirit; by assisting to obtain work, and a good place for their children as they grow up; by securing seats for them in Church and a courteous Christian welcome and friendship ; by expressions of sympathy when they lose any friend, such as furnishing a few flowers for the funeral, and asking Church people to send their carriages to a funeral to save expense.

9.　A union Mothers' meeting is desirable occasionally, if there is more than one. Also, a children's meeting should be held once or twice a year, which should be in the chapel or Sunday-school room of the Parish, or in some other central place, that the women connected with all the meetings and their children may attend. The women themselves will provide the refreshments. Before these are served, the service will be said; the text given and learned, to be recited by those remembering it at the next meeting, to whom Prayer Books and Bibles are given, and an address made by the Rector, or by the Bishop, if present. A similar general meeting held annually for the men as well as the women, at which there may be refreshments, music, and addresses, will be of great social advantage.

10.　She who undertakes such work must not be discouraged, however few attend the meeting, and very little seems to be accomplished. The benefits are not simply to the constant attendants, but to their familes and even their neighbors. It is not in vain, if some are elevated socially and improved in their temporal condition. But if any, however few, are strengthened in good habits and spiritually enlightened and learn to love the worship and service of God, and to use diligently the means of grace, though the world gives little recognition of the good done, we know that the angels in Heaven rejoice. And there is this incidental result, of inestimable value, that the Church wins the respect and ultimately the love of the masses of the people, and proves that she is catholic in her adaptability to minister effectually to all sorts and conditions of men.

11. Some organization of those employed in such work will be almost a matter of course, but should be very simple and informal and unincumbered with many rules and by-laws. Thus they will meet from time to time for mutual consultation and such advice and instruction as the Rector may desire to give. Each should report the number of visits made and the number belonging to and in attendance at the meetings, of which there will be kept a permanent record. Besides action to increase the usefulness of the Mothers' meetings, plans for various kinds of charitable effort may be matured and carried out according to the wants of the several districts and the circumstances of the Parish. A Hospital or Church Home, growing up as the need becomes apparent, will give to the workers a centre of operations, and they may become practically associated in a sisterhood. THE RECTOR WHO GIVES HIS WORKERS WHO DESERVE IT HIS ENTIRE CONFIDENCE, AND WHO SHOWS THEM THAT HE TRUSTS THEM WHILE HOLDING THEM ACCOUNTABLE, WILL ALWAYS BE REWARDED WITH THEIR LOYALTY AND DEVOTION.

VIII.

S. Luke iv, 18, 19 : The Spirit of the Lord is upon
me, because He hath anointed me to preach the Gospel
to the poor ; He hath sent me to heal the broken-
hearted, to preach deliverance to the captives and recovering of sight to the blind, to set at liberty them
that are bruised, to preach the acceptable year of the
Lord.

WHEN Jesus came back to Nazareth, where He had
been brought up, after His baptism, temptation
and full entrance upon His ministry, He went to the
synagogue and took these words as the text of His discourse. He preached such a sermon as His auditors had
never heard before. Applying the words to Himself,
assuming that the prophet had so intended, He set forth
distinctly the purpose and the nature and benefits of the
Gospel. They were all astonished at His doctrine. Often
as they may have read the text, they had been without
the slightest conception of its meaning. How often you
have read or heard it, dear brethren. The words are quite
familiar ; but do you understand it much better than
they ?

What *is* Christianity? For what purpose are you in Christ? For what purpose does the Church of Christ exist? The application our Lord made of the text is to teach us. It gives to such questions the answer. On so important an occasion as the first preaching of Jesus in the home of His youth and early manhood, He would naturally take a text from which He would strike the key note of His whole ministry. He would show once for all what was the great purpose of His coming into the world. He would proclaim what He was to be to men; what His Church was to be; what Christianity was to be; what was the meaning and end of His Gospel. If you study His life from this time onwards, until His death on Calvary, you will see that all His teaching and all His acts were in perfect accordance with His great sermon in Nazareth, and were, in fact, the practical exemplification of its meaning.

In entire harmony with His preaching, were the proofs He gave of His Messiahship in the presence of John's Disciples, who were sent to ask Him: "Art Thou He that should come, or do we look for another?" "Go and show John," said He in His all sufficient answer, "go and show John what things ye do hear and see; the blind receive their sight, the lame walk, the deaf hear, the dead are raised up, and the poor have the Gospel preached unto them, and blessed is he whosoever is not offended in Me."

Such was Christ's work. Such was His Gospel. Such

were the things which He " began both to do and teach."
Take it literally. Do not be offended at it and pervert it.
The words are plain enough. He came to do, His Church
was to do, His people were to do just these things; "to
preach the Gospel to the poor, to heal the broken-hearted,
to preach deliverance to the captives and recovering of
sight to the blind, to set at liberty them that are bruised,
to preach the acceptable year of the Lord." Do you
understand it? Do you not see that this is your work
and duty as members of the Church of Christ?

The Church of the Apostles understood it, and they
went forth into all the world to continue the work which
Christ Himself began "both to do and teach" (Acts
i, 1), and the poor, "the common people," the great
masses of mankind, the afflicted and the sorrowing, as
when Jesus preached, "heard them gladly." They dem-
onstrated that in Christ Jesus there is no distinction of
rank or of race. They brought into active operation in
all the great centres of population throughout the Roman
and Greek speaking world those spiritual forces, that
were to do away with caste, that were to renovate and
purify the life of man and of society, that were to minister to the ills and heal the maladies that flesh is heir to,
and establish the life of peace and joy upon our earth.

The Apostolic primitive Church understood it, and
finding her richest treasures in her poor, whom the Lord
had said ye have always with you, she began to fill the world

with homes, asylums, refuges and hospitals for every form of sickness, infirmity and distress. She brought health and life into the effete and decaying institutions of heathenism, abolished the barbarism, the cruelties, the dissoluteness, the shameless vices and putrid corruption which the conventionalities of civilized heathen society had sanctioned and upheld. She infused into her memberships the "enthusiasm of humanity;" made real and effective the idea of human brotherhood; lifted men up to the consciousness of their recovered freedom in Christ, and their relation to God as His children; created the Christian home and the loving ties and sweet amenities of pure domestic life; planted the germs of the Christian State and of all that is pure and good, refining and elevating in our Christian civilization. So Jesus Christ, in His Church, went forth, conquering and to conquer, and raising mankind up into His subjection, which is the ground of perfect freedom.

And to-day all that is best in our society and institutions, all the moral purity of our homes, all the love we find for man as man, the beneficence that cares for and relieves the afflicted, and the exaltation of the poor to the fellowship and privileges of men in Christ : all these things and a thousand others which distinguish us of this land and this age, are due to Christ working in and through His Church and the principles of His Revelation. The Spirit of the Lord is upon the Church as upon Him, upon her as His body, His organ, intrusted with His work, anointing her to preach the Gospel, the glad tidings of temporal and spiritual salvation to the poor, to those not favored with wealth, to those who in the sweat of their faces earn their bread ; to preach deliverance to the captives and recovering of sight to the blind, to set at liberty them that are bruised, to preach the acceptable year of the Lord, the jubilee of freedom and peace.

In some measure all this is done through the Church, though many of us who are her members and agents of her work, are ignorant of her character, and obstructive rather than helpful to her mission. But what might she not do if we, her members, were all faithful to our real " vocation and ministry " as Christians !

Why are we not? Doubtless for many reasons, but largely this : Because we have somehow lost the true conception of what Christianity really is and what is the Church's mission and work. Many have come to make Christianity almost altogether a doctrinal system, and so the Church, so far as committed by them to the preaching of barren speculations without the heat and warmth of love, has alienated multitudes of the benevolent in whom Christ's Spirit was working, though in outside and irregular channels, a truer and diviner life.

Added to this, the Gospel which was first preached to the poor and the rude and unlettered masses, came to pervade all conditions and to equalize all ranks of men. The rich and the highly cultured received it, and their wealth and culture were subsidized by it and became in the hands of the Church, as was most meet, potent instrumentalities in her missionary work and the moral and spiritual elevation of the people. But by and by, little by little, they began to appropriate it to themselves as if it were their exclusive possession, and the poor, the less favored classes, were left to grope their way uncared for and undirected in the spiritual darkness and gloom of sin.

Whatever the explanation, in our own day, among us in this city, the Gospel in its true character is not preached and brought home, as the Lord intended, to the poor, the captives, the bruised, the broken-hearted, the great masses of the people. Whatever other reasons there may be for the prevailing indifference to this paramount duty, these at least may be regarded as practically among the greatest. It has somehow come to be the popular opinion: first, that Christianity consists only or chiefly of its doctrines; and secondly, that it is the possession and property of what are called by a miserable misnomer "the better classes." These two misconceptions are working most disastrous consequences.

The importance of sound doctrine cannot be exaggerated. But we must distinguish. What is sound doctrine? All doctrines that are essential in Christianity are summed up in the ancient and universal Creeds. And these are primarily and for the most part *facts* of the Gospel history.

Rightly understood, all the doctrines of the Christian faith, as the Church Cathecism teaches us, are contained in the Apostles' Creed. This faith and Creed all men are sworn to in their baptism ; and all that *is* or ever *was* or *can be* required of them in becoming members of the Church, is the faith of the Creed of the Apostles, interpreted and understood in the light of the so-called Creed of Nicæa, to be thenceforward exemplified in holy and consistent lives.

But in the last few hundred years the idea of the Creed has been indefinitely extended and strangely perverted. Multiplied and interminable confessions of faith have been drawn up by good and devout men, embodying many abstract theological opinions, colored by the prevailing philosophy and metaphysics of the times of their production. These, by a strange perversion, are taken to be *Creeds.* And so Christianity is by many conceived to be but little else than dogmas. Amidst the disputes of theologians on points of opinion altogether outside of what is essential to salvation, the real Creed, the true Faith, is by many forgotten, and the beneficent work of the Church in saving men from sin and elevating and blessing them in spirit, soul and body, is lost sight of. The Redeemer of man is shunned, the Saviour of man is rejected, through ignorance for which Christians are responsible, and through prejudice which is natural, which can only be removed by the Church showing herself to be Christ's body and living representative, and doing the work for which He came into the world.

Consider the innumerable treatises upon Christianity. They are almost all in explanation of its doctrines. One would scarcely suspect from them that there was anything more in it than doctrines ; and yet a large part of these "doctrines" is matter of dispute. Consider the tens of thousands of sermons preached and published. They are mostly of the same character. So at least it appears to those of whom we speak.

There is, dear brethren, a remedy. The Church constantly presents it. For doctrine, that is, of faith and not of mere opinion, she bids us come back of all this literature to the old Creed of Christendom, which expresses the soul's loyalty, faith and fealty, to God, Father, Son and Holy Spirit ; the facts of the Church, Christ's Body, of pardon and peace in Him, of Resurrection, Life and Immortality. Here is what we want, what the heart of man requires of doctrine, always the same and forever true, like the Lord Himself, yesterday, to-day and forever. Of the high themes of "Fate, Foreknowledge, Knowledge Absolute," in which acute disputants find themselves "in endless mazes lost," leave all that where it belongs, to the sphere of opinion, and so of the innumerable doctrines, true or false, outside the faith of the old Creed, that divides Christians into parties and sects; and then come back to the old and true Gospel as the text presents it, as the Lord in His life on earth, going about doing good, exemplified it, and as the Church of all ages has been commissioned to proclaim it, and to carry it out, and make it effectual in the redemption and salvation of the world.

And as for that other perversion, that Christianity is for a class or classes, that it is in any degree a caste religion, if you have, any of you, even for a moment, even in thoughtlessness and unconsciousness, entertained any such idea, repent of it, repudiate it, get rid of it, despise it as it deserves.

To the poor the Gospel is preached. Preach, then, in your lives, in all your actions, the Gospel of universal love, and sympathy, and kindness; the Gospel that confers all spiritual and temporal blessings; the Gospel that refines and elevates all who receive it in its saving power; the Gospel that binds all men, of all classes and conditions, in bonds of fraternal affection, in which there is neither Jew nor Greek, Barbarian, Scythian, bond nor free, but all are one in Christ Jesus,—the Gospel of the Kingdom, the Church of Jesus Christ. He took upon Himself our common human nature. He lived here in poverty. His associates, disciples and Apostles were tax collectors and fishermen, and men of the people. He bore our sicknesses and infirmities. He died for our sins on the Cross of Shame. His greatest Apostle could say, writing to the Church at Corinth, planted in the midst of Greek refinement, culture, elegance, luxury and dissipation: " Ye see your calling, brethren, how that not many mighty, not many wise men after the flesh, not many noble, are called." You know the passage. I need not quote further.

What, then, is the practical conclusion of the whole matter?

First get the true realization in your minds and hearts of what Christianity really is, what it means to be Christians, what is your "vocation and ministry," how you are to be Christ-like in conduct and in life; how you are to have in all the depths of your being that *love for men as men*, that brought Jesus Christ into our world, and to give His life in sacrifice for man.

And then having the mind that was in Christ Jesus, show it. Exemplify it in word and deed. Prove it by the way in which you honor, and fellowship, and welcome the poor who come to this Cathedral to worship and to hear the Gospel preached. Go out into the highways and compel them to come in; organize the work of gathering and teaching them. Give it your time, your thought, your money. Show to all the people such kindness, such tender, sympathetic interest as they can quickly see comes from loving hearts, and to your own spiritual growth and blessedness make the Church grow and the Word of God to have free course and be glorified.

IX.

THE USE OF GRACE A MEANS OF GRACE.

2 Cor. ix, 10 : Now he that ministereth seed to the sower, both minister bread for your food and multiply your seed sown and increase the fruits of your righteousness.

IT is very important that we should not take too restricted a view of the means of grace. The two great Sacraments which are "generally necessary to salvation," are rightly regarded as pre-eminently means of grace. But in so teaching, it is not meant to deny that Confirmation and other Apostolic or divinely instituted rites or ordinances have their own proper and especial grace connected with their right administration and reception. In fact, there are in Christianity many outward and visible signs of inward spiritual grace given unto us. Our Lord, on various occasions, used such signs for temporary purposes, when He would bestow both gifts of healing and the faith to appropriate the accompanying spiritual blessing. Nature herself has means of grace to those who know how to receive and profit by them. Many an object, many a scene does she present which may be fitted to raise the heart in thankfulness to God and to call forth praises to the bountiful Giver of all good. But besides those means of grace, which are sacraments or sacramental in their nature, in which the grace is, as it were, outwardly presented and bestowed by its Author through the means of His choice or ordinance, a receptive state of heart being the condition of its appropriation, there are others which are of first importance in which *we* are active, in which we co-operate with God, in which our devout earnestness brings a large increase of grace, being the necessary condition of its reception. Such are prayer and meditation, and the hearing and study of the Word of God, and exercises of penitence, and confession of sin. The grace comes while we are struggling towards it and striving to obtain it. Without the use of such means of grace, no others can avail us. Prayer, for example, is an exercise of faith, and the very exercise brings an increase of faith. In prayer for any desired blessing, there is trust that it will be given, there is the effort involved to obtain it, and the repose of mind and heart, the confidence and satisfaction which are pre-eminently fitted for its reception. The desire, the seeking and the consequent labor, do not indeed insure the answer, except so far as this comes as a reflex influence. It is God from Whom proceed all blessings. But the expectant attitude, the earnest seeking, the strenuous effort are indispensable conditions. These means of grace have much of the subjective element. The gift of blessing which God bestows through these means has ordinarily no

outward sign by which it is both symbolized and con-
veyed.

My purpose is to speak of a necessary means of grace,
which is too seldom considered such. It is not sacramental. It may be distinguished from the several means
of which the various acts of penitence and self-discipline
are examples. It is more nearly allied to prayer, for
sincere prayer should inevitably lead to it. It is WORK
FOR CHRIST, zealous, distinctive Christian effort that I
refer to. That to pray is to labor, and to labor is to pray,
is a truth well recognized in the Christian economy. But
it is seldom practically realized. Prayer is too often but
a formal and perfunctory exercise. Work is the natural
outgoing of the heart that truly prays. Labors for Christ
are the completion or complement of prayer. If we do not
earnestly seek that which we pray for, our mere prayers
will be ineffectual. How does the prayer of faith remove
mountains? Faith gives the assurance that the mountains, whatever they are, must and shall be removed, and
calls forth the effort necessary to remove them. God rewards such faith by blessing the labor and insuring its
success.

In the text, the special effort alluded to, is giving for
the cause of Christ. God blesses such sowing not only to
those for whom it is done, but also in the harvest of
blessings which the sower must reap in the end. But
giving is but a single branch of the general subject of

labor for Christ and His Church. He who gives cheerfully
and works cheerfully on behalf of the spread of the Gospel and the extension and edification of the Church of
God, finds an increase of blessing in his own soul. The
fruits of righteousness are abundantly increased and
matured. His life and character exhibit them. They
enter into the formation of character. They are garnered
up and become a permanent, inalienable possession.

The principle in which the truth is grounded which I
wish to bring out distinctly, is that the use or improvement
of grace is itself a means of grace. Everything given or
done for Christ is but the proper result of grace received.
It is not only commanded. Not only is it a necessary part
of Christian obedience. It is the outworking of faith
which is the gift of God. It is prompted and inspired by
the Spirit of Christ. It is the strength which cometh from
above in which it is accomplished.

Let us see, then, how the use of grace is a means of
grace; how every work done for Christ and for Christ's
sake, strengthens the doer with new strength from above.
Thus we shall learn how true it is that Almighty God, Who
supplies seed to the sower and bread for the eating, will
supply and multiply your seed sown and increase the
fruits of your righteousness.

We might expect this to be true from the analogies
which are constantly under our observation. It is universally true that *use* gives strength and facility. Physic-

ally, the use of any class of muscles gives them power and dexterity. We see this in the acquisition of all trades and mechanic arts. I need only refer to the strength of the right arm, the dexterity of the fingers of the skillful hand, the unerring precision of the practiced eye, the suppleness of limbs by which feats of agility are done which astonish us. Everybody knows how surely " practice makes perfect." It is the same with all mental exercise. The use of faculties develops and strengthens them. The possibility of all education depends upon the fact that use gives enlargement of capacity, strength and facility. Thus prolonged and strenuous attention is the secret of great accomplishment in every department of study. By exercise memory becomes retentive, the perceptions quick, the judgment sure, the understanding strong, the will indomitable in action. So it is in every branch of special study, or practice, as music, sculpture, painting. So, too, with the powers by which beauty in nature or art is appreciated.

From such analogies, which might, of course, be multiplied to any extent, it should be expected that the same or a similar law would be operative in the various kinds of work and duty of which the Church of God is the sphere. It might be expected that the constant acting in faith would give strength to faith; that love would be intensified as it is concentrated upon objects that call it forth and employ its energies; that hope would become as the

anchor of the soul, sure and steadfast, as it is cast within
the veil of the Sanctuary, and that all the fruits of the
spirit would grow and abound in proportion to the degree
of their culture. For, in addition to the natural effect
of use to develop and strengthen the faculties, in addition
to the confirming of habits of action by exercise, the
special grace of God is promised as the enabling power of
every act of obedience, every exercise of a right disposition. Not only does the appetite grow by what it feeds
on, not only do the desires, the affections, the voluntary
powers gain by use in intensity, in scope, in capacity,
but as their exercise depends upon grace prompting and
co-operating, and as all the grace needed for use is
promised and bestowed, so new grace will be required and
given as the capacity for it enlarges, as the powers of the
soul are expanded. Hence increase of use secures increase
of grace. And hence the *ratio* of the increase of power
to him who is employed in doing good after the example of
Christ and in obedience to Him, is, so to speak, geometrical.
It is a process of constant multiplication, not simply the
addition of a fixed quantity. For there are two laws
that are operative : the law of natural increase of capacity
and power by the use of the faculties, and the spiritual
law by which grace is always sufficient, and is given the
more, as more is capable of being improved by the growing and enlarged capacities of the spiritual nature.
Hence the babe in Christ, or the child in respect of Chris-

tian growth, using all the grace or the divinely imparted power that is possible, requires far less than can be appropriated and used by one who is reaching a maturity of godliness and approximating to the measure of the stature of Christian manhood. We ought not, therefore, to be surprised when we see examples of saintly men and women by whom labors for Christ and His Church, which call for extraordinary powers of zeal, energy and endurance, are successfully prosecuted. There is, indeed, no work which is so difficult, if it be acceptable to Christ, if love prompts and demands it, if faith can conceive it possible and undertake it, for the accomplishment of which abundant grace will not be given. There are no capacities for effort which grace will not fill, no powers so great that grace can not enlarge and energize them.

Let us look at the subject a little more in detail. Take the case to which the text has primary reference, that of generous, abundant sacrifice in the way of giving for Christ and for the Church, especially of giving to the extent that involves real self-denial and sacrifice. You sow the seeds of charity by bestowment of your bounties upon others. Suppose it to be for the relief of suffering. See the reward in the good result and the gratitude and love by which you are more than repaid. But more than this. See your own spiritual advancement. You are a certain degree less selfish than before. You are a perceptible degree more compassionate. You are more like your Master, Who went about doing good and gave His life, every moment of it, for our unspeakable advantage. Your dis- position to give has been intensified. By the grace of God you are larger and greater in one of the chief elements of Christian manliness.

Suppose it to be for the spread of the Gospel. Your little gift, all you can bestow, enough to require that you should deny yourself something which otherwise you might have thought indispensable, accompanied with prayer, as it must and always will be if you are in earnest, will be the means, it may be, of saving a soul from death. It may help most materially, though it be in itself little— for the aggregate of many *littles* makes the *great*—to advance Christ's kingdom in the world. How much better you are for the consciousness that you have been working with Christ, working to carry out the objects for which He gave His life. How much you are exalted in the sphere of being by the companionship to which your Lord admits you.

But besides this, your interest in the cause for which you pray and give is increased thereby, just as your love for a friend is enhanced by what you have done and suf- fered for him. You are measurably re-endowed or newly endowed with grace. You are more disposed and more enabled to give, and pray, and labor for objects to which your heart has become more devoted. So it is that he who ministereth seed to the sower and bread for the eating hath increased and multiplied your seed sown and increased the fruits of your righteousness.

And if this kind of giving is frequent and habitual, see how surely you will grow in grace thereby. You will come to rejoice rather than complain of opportunities to do good, and calls upon your charity. Your love will the more abound. Your zeal will be quickened. Your energies will reach a key of steady tension which will not let you flag or give way to the selfish love of ease, or pleasure, or money, or yield to outward difficulties and discouragements. And so the old paradox of Solomon's proverb is made plain and consistent: "There is that scattereth and yet increaseth, and there is that withholdeth more than is meet, but it tendeth to poverty."

And as it is with giving, so it is also with working, for the two things are not so essentially different as is often imagined. In fact, labor is represented by money. All wealth is the product of labor and the intelligence employed therein. Everything is valuable in the ratio of the labor it costs and the ability that directs or is given to the labor. If gold were a common metal and could be mined with as little difficulty as lead or copper, its value would be reduced accordingly. It is a general principle of the older Political Economy that labor is the measure of all values. If we must modify this by adding to labor, mind, ability, intelligence, that makes labor fruitful, it does not alter the principle. Hence, to give the labor of a day, and to him who cannot do this, the wages of a day's labor, are equivalent. Some must give work. Some must give money. The money will employ the laborers. But in such case the money must be given not for praise, not with indifference, not as a superfluity, not as costing nothing, but with a sense of what it is worth and what it can do, with real interest and prayer for the blessing of God to accompany it.

Now, this is the law. Use gives strength. Improvement of grace, in action accordant with its prompting, results in increase of grace and capacity of accomplishment. "To him that hath and of consequence useth what he hath, to him shall be given, and he shall have abundance, while from him that hath not shall be taken away that which he hath, or seemeth to have." He to whom were given ten talents and who had the grace to use them, gained ten other talents besides. He who had one talent, and hid it in the earth, had his one talent taken from him. You who have given some portion of your time to God in labors on behalf of the ignorant, the unconverted, or the poor and suffering, have no doubt felt yourselves growing into a higher type of manhood. Every act of goodness prompted by grace, has been to you a means of grace. Every good resolve the Spirit of God has helped you to make, has been attended with the grace for its fulfillment. When a man who has wandered away from God comes to himself, and says, "I will arise and go to my Father," and does at once arise and set his face heavenward and begins to act accordingly, he will find that he will have the strength to do it, however impossible it may have seemed before. "Stretch forth thy hand," said the Lord to the man whose hand was withered. The faith came with the word, to make the effort, and with the effort the strength came that made the obedience easy and the cure effectual. So he or she who undertakes to teach in the Sunday-school or the Bible class, or by diligent, systematic visiting, to gather the uncared-for into the Church of God, to conduct a Mothers' meeting or a Cottage lecture, to do hospital work, to visit the sick and give relief and prayers and consolation, or to do any of the works by which the Church is edified and extended, and souls added to the Lord, will find such labors growing more and more easy and delightful. What was at first done ill, is by and by done well. What was at first a task, becomes a pleasure. Perseverance conquers all difficulties. The secret is that the use of grace gives larger measures of grace and strength. Not only is this plainly taught in the Word of God, but all experience verifies it.

Such, dear brethren, is the law. Work in grace is a means of grace. It is a means of such high value and efficacy that all other means without this may be ineffectual. What is prayer without interest in what you pray for, without effort, whenever practicable, to obtain that which you ask of God? What is prayer without work?

Of what avail would be the Sacrament without prayer? What would be the Word of God to one who never prays? Prayer and work are inseparable. Prayer and work are conditions of continuing in grace, and of all growth in grace. See, then, your encouragement. You who are endeavoring to do your duty in the Church of God, earnestly striving to do Christ's work, go on in this good way. It is the way of happiness here. It is your sure training for eternal blessedness. In due season you shall reap, if you faint not. Therefore be not weary in well doing. He who ministereth seed to the sower and bread for sustenance will increase and multiply your seed sown and increase the fruits of your righteousness.

X.

GOD'S GIFTS TO THOSE WHO GIVE.

2 Cor. ix, 8 :   God is able to make all grace abound towards you, that ye, having all sufficiency in all things, may abound to every good work.

THE subject S. Paul is here emphasizing is liberal giving. He commends the Christians at Corinth for all they had done and encourages them to do more, on the ground that he who soweth sparingly shall reap sparingly, and he who soweth bountifully shall reap also bountifully. They were not rich in this world's goods.   Not yet had God called into His Church the rich, the noble, the mighty.   If any had been rich, they had probably done as did Barnabas the son of Consolation, at Jerusalem, and many others, of whom we are told that they sold their possessions and goods and brought the money to the Apostles for the charitable work of the Church.

It must seem strange to those who make money the measure of all good things, to hear S. Paul speaking to these poor people as "being enriched in everything to all bountifulness," and always having all sufficiency in all things.   And yet every one having any experience of life can see that it is, indeed, possible to have great earthly riches and yet to be "poor and miserable, and blind and naked." Any thoughtful person can see that a bare sufficiency for subsistence, earned from day to day, with resignation, contentment, peace of mind, love of God, and love of our neighbor, and ready sympathy with all joys and sorrows, is infinitely preferable to the greatest wealth, if with it there must be the miser's covetousness and heartlessness, the indifference which the rich not seldom manifest to other's wants, and the cool selfishness with which they sometimes exact the services of others as their due, without even the poor recompense of thanks. To test the real value of anything we may possess, we must consider how it will serve us in extremity, what solace it can bring us in sickness and pain, and sorrow and bereavement. Then it is that the true riches of the heart and mind show their manifest pre-eminence. Superfluous wealth, wealth with which friends have not been made by its proper use, can bring no remedy in the terrible sicknesses of the soul, which it so often causes or aggravates, when it is sought and loved and held for its own sake. Who has not seen men going down to the grave in sufferings aggravated beyond measure by the cares which their wealth occasioned, and yet clinging to it with a grasp so tenacious that death could alone relax it, and thus dying in misery, having no treasures laid up safely where they will be forever needed and might be enjoyed to all eternity!

It was Christ who said, " how hardly shall they that have riches enter into the kingdom of heaven." And yet that " all things are possible with God." If they do enter therein by withdrawing the heart from their worldly possessions, esteeming them only for the good uses that may be made of them, rejoicing to do as Christ did, Who " though He was rich, yet for our sakes He became poor," and so, like Him, scattering blessings around on every side by giving for His sake in something of His Spirit of sacrifice, Who gave all for us, even His life, then, indeed, they may be worthy members and obtain honorable position and glorious rewards. Glad would any one be to be able to do all the good that might be in his heart. There is no prayer which should be made more constantly and with a more sincere and earnest devotion by any one to whom riches are in possession or in prospect, than this : O Lord, if with wealth must come a hard, selfish, ungrateful heart, a heart that would let money outweigh any human suffering or want that would seek relief at my hands, and a narrowness and meanness of spirit that would justify the scornful reproaches it generally receives, then let me be poor. Take from me the occasions of so great temptation, and suffer me not to sink into such moral degeneracy. Let me not be rich, unless it be without the love of money, which is the root of all evil. Let me not be rich, unless I can still enter into Thy kingdom and use all I have for Christ and His cause. Let me not be rich, unless I can be also rich towards God, rich in good works, rich in abundant blessings to men. What right-thinking person would not, if he had the remotest prospect of more than a competence, make such a prayer the expression of the deepest desires of his heart?

We can now easily see that the persons addressed by S. Paul in the text, though poor in a worldly acceptation, might be rich in a sense far higher and more true. And, therefore, it was natural and consistent that they should be said to have always all sufficiency, all that they needed, so as to be able always to abound in every good work. The words were to them a precious promise. Having a willingness to do good, a readiness of mind and heart to give as God should prosper them, it should follow of consequence, that God would make all grace abound towards them, so that they should always have sufficient of all really good things, for themselves, for the needs of others, for the cause of Christ and the Church.

What is the meaning of the promise? It is God's guarantee of a sufficiency of all good things, temporal and spiritual, to those who give themselves to Him, and include in the gift of themselves, to make it real, their energies, their means of influence, all their power of doing good, "not grudgingly nor of necessity." Can any Christian doubt it? Does not the whole Bible assume its truth? It is Solomon's axiom (Prov. xi, 24, 25). It is the teaching of the prophets (Mal. iii, 10). The

Apostles do but reiterate in varied language a most fundamental principle of the Gospel. The *use* of the talents
intrusted brings accumulation. " The liberal soul shall
be made fat." They who are ready to give and glad to
distribute, shall have all good things abounding unto
them.

The ground of this truth is in God's promise and God's
ability. Do you believe in Him? He is able to make all
grace abound towards you. All grace is for corporate use.
All His grace given, all that He intrusts to you, is to enable
you to abound in all good works towards your fellows.
The sufficiency you have is not for yourselves. It is given
that you may be instruments for conferring blessings upon
others.

Here, then, is offered to all men the greatest wealth that
we can possess. It is in the grace of generosity, the love
of doing good and making others happy, the desire and
the ability to be instruments of the highest service to God
and our fellow men, in the promotion of the cause of Christ.

Get wealth, then; accumulate property, lands, stocks,
money, creaturely comforts, but set not your heart upon
any of these things. Use them for the ends for which
they are given you. Joys unspeakable come from doing
good with a lavish hand, in utter forgetfulness of self. If
a man is bent only on getting and keeping in all possible
ways as much property as he can, it is not possible even
for Almighty God to make him rich in his feeling; rich in

the priceless happiness that comes from doing the utmost possible of good in the world; rich in the gratitude of a Christian community, and the approval of God and man. If selfishness and covetousness be unrepressed and even intensified by long-indulged habits, it is impossible there should be the blessedness that only follows giving on a large and generous scale. What are we to say of those rich people who deny themselves habitually the means for cultivating the refinements and amenities of life, content to remain in ignorance, without appreciation of the good, the true, the beautiful, in man's works and in God's world, because they cannot spare the money which they prefer to pile up in useless accumulations for somebody to fight about, or to waste improvidently after they are gone; of those who have lands that perhaps they never saw, which they will not sell nor improve and occupy because increasing in value, the taxes and necessary expenses upon which are paid grudgingly, with a distressing feeling of poverty and inability; of those who strain every nerve to make more, using all their income and all they can borrow for coveted investments, and then say, believing it to be true, that they have nothing to give for the work of the Church, nor even enough for the necessary expenses to which their social position and their place in the Church compels them? These are the poor people in every community. God gives worldly prosperity and makes it a curse and a punishment to those who will not understand that it is from Him, and that He has chosen them to the stewardships of its use in His service. The punishment comes by the law of cause and effect. Any selfish love, especially of any thing material and temporal, like the perishable treasures of this world, produces in the heart a contractedness, a belittling of all manly and generous impulses, and a poverty of soul which makes its possessor an object of pity to all good people, and of contempt to those who can not pity them.

But God enriches the generous and noble-hearted, so that the more they give the more they have to give, the more good they do, the more they have to enjoy, and the stronger their will to abound in giving and in all good works. In two ways He may enrich them: He gives them temporal prosperity and makes it a personal and general blessing. There are indeed cases in which bad, selfish people are greatly prospered in worldly things. But the noble, generous Christian who uses all God gives in the highest and best ways, is usually prospered the more. That this may be so will not be doubted by those who know that God rules this world by His Providence, that He gives the power to get wealth, and withholds no good thing from His children. Again, many selfish men overreach themselves by their grasping character, and are tempted to ventures which are indistinguishable from gambling, and are not honest, and so lose both money and reputation. The habits that are best cultivated by a man who fears and serves God and trusts and loves his fellow men, are favorable to success in life. Thrift, industry and honest dealing are Christian virtues. Ability, prudence, energy and perseverance seldom fail even of earthly recompense.   Besides, Christian principle will restrain a man from all those questionable speculations which so often end in ruin, and will prevent the bad habits of self-indulgence to which those who think only of themselves are liable, and which so generally prove disastrous.   It would be easy to follow out the natural causes of the prosperity of those who always do right, and of the failure of those whose short-sighted selfishness and over-eagerness to be rich, leads them into temptation and a snare. But facts are better than theories, and it is the fact, taking the words in the most literal sense, that God is able to make His grace and favor abound towards you who love to do good with what you have, and to use it generously in His service, so that ye, always having all sufficiency in all things, may abound unto every good work.   Thus to him that hath shall be given, who generously and rightly useth what he hath, while from him that hath not—because he hoards and will not use it—from him shall be taken away even that which he hath.

But the highest grace is spiritual.   What to us is a sufficiency depends upon our disposition.   If you should give for some greatly desired and noble end, for which you had been eagerly planning, one-half or all of your income, and even so much of your property as to leave yourself with little or nothing but your hands, your brains and your love of work, you might still feel that you were rich. When Barnabas and his fellow disciples had given all they had to the Apostles for their work, do you suppose they felt poor? Do you suppose the Good Samaritan felt impoverished by the cost of the oil and wine with which he bound up the wounds of the man who had fallen among thieves, and the charges for his board and nursing and medical treatment till his recovery? Do you think the poor widow who gave all her living into the treasury of God, or the woman who poured the precious ointment upon the head and feet of the Saviour, felt that they had not in consequence greater riches than before? No, brethren, the money God gives into our care is for us to use for Him. It is of no value except as it is used in doing good to ourselves and others. The true wealth is that of the heart, and mind, and soul. And every one who gives in the full measure of Gospel privilege will experience this in a joy which the world could not give and cannot take away.

Not until men of wealth learn to acknowledge and meet its responsibilities, can the Church do the work that now presses upon her towards the toiling masses of men. The signs are not wanting that presage untold trouble to the men of capital, which might so easily be averted would the Christian men of wealth learn at once how to use it. The real love of men acting itself out in true Christian beneficence, if generally prevailing, would solve all difficulties which confront us. The Church would soon be the effective agent in the amelioration of all temporal as well as spiritual wants, if only those who give themselves to God would but, with themselves, give all they have and are, as the Gospel they profess requires. The great, the imperative demand of the Church at this time is to bring not only all the members, but especially her rich and well-to-do people, to the realization of their accountability in the use of their means; to open their eyes to see that they are not generally as yet giving for God, for the Church's work, more than an infinitesimally small portion of what is required of them, and of what they must give to avert disaster from themselves, and from the Church the reproach of failure.

XI.

S. Luke viii, 38, 39: Now the man out of whom the devils were departed, besought Him that he might be with Him. But Jesus sent him away, saying: return to thine own house and show how great things God hath done unto thee. And he went his way and published throughout the whole city how great things Jesus had done unto him.

THERE is difficulty in understanding the miracle of which the text is the sequel. There is a "border land" between sanity and insanity. There is a psychological region on the confines of mind and feeling which has not been well explored. There is a possibility of a double consciousness. Thoughts may find utterance through our vocal organs that are not truly our own. There is a part of our nature which is liable to intrusion by evil spirits. As wickedness may possess a man, so the demons of wickedness and of uncleanness may invade his nature and control him. And through Jesus Christ, the great healing and restorative power for man's salvation, such demon spirits may be cast out.

What relation there may be between such demon spirits and the dumb, swinish nature, we do not know.

As man is a *microcosm* of the great world without him, as his nature includes, sums up and comprehends all inferior natures, it is not improbable that men and beasts may be alike possessed by alien powers in the parts of their natures which they have in common, or in which they have a likeness or affinity. Until we know a great deal more than we do at present of that part of man's nature that borders on the brutish and of what in brute beasts is in nearest likeness to the sensibilities and appetences of man, we have no right to say that the fact recorded in the Gospel is impossible. We must take the Gospel facts as true, as we do all other facts, until the contrary is proved. If we should give credence to no facts that we cannot understand in their causes, we should believe and know very little indeed. None are skeptics in everything. If they were, they could not live in human society. They could transact no business with their fellow men. Let us be careful how we deny what it is impossible for us to say is not actual and real.

It is not necessary to dwell further upon the miracle of the casting out of the legion of devils from the man so terribly possessed, as read to-day in the Gospel. It was a work of mercy as easy to our Lord as any work of His omnipotence. It is the after-demeanor of the man so wonderfully restored, it is his natural request and the Lord's answer, and his subsequent conduct, that contain the lessons we are to learn to-day.

A passing word is enough to give to the owners of the swine that had met with such a fearful end. There are people now-a-days who are not unlike them. *They* were not moved with gratitude to the Great Deliverer who had perfectly restored the poor sufferer. *They* did not rejoice when they saw him sitting and clothed, and in his right mind. *They* cared nothing for this wonderful work of mercy at which Angels rejoiced. *They* felt no concern in the redemptive work of Christ upon the bodies and the souls of men. They were absorbed in their selfishness. In view of their own pecuniary loss they had no thought nor sympathy for another's gain. Therefore they were amazed and affrighted. Their property, unlawful if they were Jews, had perished. *Therefore* Jesus was a dangerous person to have among them. They began at once vehemently to beseech Him that He would depart out of their coasts. So men reject Christ and His blessed work ! So their selfishness makes them blind to the most beneficent work that is going on in this world, the extension of Christ's Kingdom and the salvation of men.

Not so with this poor, healed demoniac. He clings to Jesus. He feels that he cannot leave Him. He prays that he may remain with Him. He desires to enter into the ship with Him and pass over to the other side, to join the disciples, out of and away from this semi-heathen country of Perea. He would go with Jesus and demonstrate his love and gratitude by his life-long devotion and service.

We cannot doubt but that the Saviour was deeply moved by such evidences of love and faithfulness. But what answer did He give to him? Surely at first it must surprise us. He said, No, I have other work for you here in your own country. Go home to your kindred and friends and tell them what things the Lord hath done for you, and how He hath had compassion on you.

These selfish, unsympathizing people of Gadara certainly needed a Missionary. The Lord would place this devoted follower where he could do the most good. Where should this be, but in his own home, among his relatives, friends and acquaintances, who had known him in his terrible madness, to whom he had been an object of terror and dread?

The man's home and surroundings were wicked. Yet Christ bade him stay there. He had not chosen that home, but it was his. He must remain in it. We are not to seek scenes of danger and temptation, but being in them are there to glorify God by our work for Him. The highest duty is generally that which lies nearest to us. The Christian must, at our Lord's bidding, stay and be the leaven to Christianize and the salt to make and keep pure the place and neighborhood of his abode.

What did the man reply to Jesus? Did he remonstrate? Did he decline to fulfil the Lord's bidding? Did he still insist on remaining with Him? Timid as he might well be, fearful as he might be to trust himself alone, and needing, as he felt he needed, the presence and the companionship of Jesus, and doubtful as he might well be whether he could do any good for the cause of Christ in his old home and country, still he is ready. He does not for a moment hesitate. He thinks no more of self. In faith he obeys, doubtless feeling sure that his Lord knew best where he should be and where his presence and work would be most effective for His cause. And so he goes home immediately to his kindred and friends and shows what the Lord had done for him, and he publishes it abroad in all Decapolis, the ten cities of Perea. Poor a subject as you would think him out of which to make a Missionary, his ministry was most effectual.

I need not dwell upon the manner in which his ministry is performed. What must have been the effect of his very presence, in perfect sanity and health? See him at home and going in and out among his people. His countenance is expressive only of love. His eyes, that once flashed forth the fires of madness, now return the look of affection. He is calm, collected, entirely himself, and he ascribes all the glory and praise to Christ. What a sermon was this! How powerful to convince and to persuade! But he does more than merely to stand, clothed and in his right mind, among his people. He goes about preaching Jesus. All who have known him, and many others, hear from his lips the story of his healing and salvation.

Here, then, brethren, is an example for you. This man is what every Christian must be. He only does what is the plain duty of every one who is saved in Christ. He preaches to you to-day a most effective sermon. Listen to its teaching, impress it upon your hearts. The message to you is " Go and do thou likewise." Obey as he did, the voice of the Lord, through Whom you are redeemed and saved. Show yourselves to be Christ's by your lives of soberness, righteousness and godliness. Tell alike by your conduct and your fitly spoken words what the Lord hath done for you. Let the power of your example and your life of active goodness, and the positive influence of your untiring efforts by word and deed, bring those with whom you come in contact nearer to Christ and to His healing grace in His Church.

Let those who profess to be saved in Christ, prove it to the world by their lives, their conduct and their teaching. Let them see to it that among their nearest kindred, in their homes, in the circle of their friends and acquaintances, among their neighbors and those whom they meet in the relations of business and of society, they shall fulfil the Lord's command, and tell and show forth what the Lord hath done for them, the power of His healing grace, the moulding influence of His love, making them Christ-like in character.

There is no principle more fundamental in Christianity than this: That every one who is a Christian must seek to make others Christians.   Christian love is diffusive. If it be in you, it must constrain you.   It must determine your conduct.   It must form your character.

How is it with you, brethren?   You are in the Church. You are baptized into Christ, into His death, His sacrifice. Is His love in your heart?   Is His Spirit yours?   Does it actuate you?   Does it make you like Him?   Does it lead you to follow Him?   Does it impel you to give your lives for others?   Does it constrain you to do His work, and give your active help in carrying on that redemptive process by which Jesus Christ is saving men and repairing, restoring the ruins sin has made in this sinful world?

It was said to me not long since by one of your most thoughtful and influential business men : "This congregation is dying of selfishness.   Its work is all for itself.   It thinks only of its own comfort and enjoyment."   This is a terrible arraignment.   Is there truth in it?   How much of truth is there in it?   God forbid that it should be so bad as this.   If it have any grounds at all, God forbid that it should so continue for a day.

If you resent such an imputation, try at least to understand how any one could have made it.   The criticisms of friends should be helpful.

I must not take the position of an accuser.   The congregation ought to be as its individuals.   If the members are worthy Christian livers and active Christian workers, the congregation should be the same, and the corporate life of the body should manifest itself in the Christian activities to which the individuals are pledged and should be devoted. And this corporate action should be resistless. The corporate life should manifest itself in effective organization to make the work in the highest degree successful in the greatest good of men, to the greater glory of God.

Let us lay down an imperative Christian duty — a duty that rests on a most essential principle of the Gospel. We can thus test ourselves. We can see wherein we are delinquent, and what we have to amend. I speak now only of duty about which there is no question among Christians. It is the *duty* of every one of us and of all of us combined to evangelize, to Christianize the people around us. This means the people of this city, of all classes not yet reached by the Gospel. It means the people of all the wards and all the suburbs of this town, and the surrounding country. It means the people of this State, of this Diocese, and of the country at large. It means the people of these United States, and of the whole world. More than it is a duty to support the government, the state schools, and the state institutions for the common good, it is the duty of all Christian people to support the Church and her agencies for the evangelization of our home, our neighborhood, our country, and the world. And such support involves personal activity, in zealous, devoted, self-sacrificing exertion. If there are many who cannot bear their part in the Missionary work incumbent upon them, by personal service, they are not therefore exempted from the obligation. The soldier who cannot fight must employ a substitute. They who cannot go into the field must provide the support of others. It requires money for this. The propagation of the Gospel in the extension of the Church at home and abroad is largely a question of money. And offerings of money are the most ordinary and practical proof of interest. Under the present arrangements in the business world and the social organism, not to give with free-handed liberality for the missions and charities of the Church, is to be, like the Gadarenes, blind, indifferent to the power and beneficence of Christ's Gospel. It is equivalent to doing nothing whatever towards accomplishing the end for which Christ came into this world, and to lose all share in His work and His rewards.

Now, what are *you* doing? How much are *you* giving for Missions, in the Parish, in the city, in the jurisdiction, in the domestic and foreign field? Must the answer be, almost nothing? Must you make such answer to yourselves? When the exigencies of the work demand one-tenth, or one-half, or for some even the whole of your income, must you confess that you are only, year by year, giving nothing that has called for any thought, or occasioned the least degree of sacrifice? Are *you* Christians, then, and do you expect for yourselves spiritual growth and health, and for your Church prosperity and success? Under the law of Christ's Kingdom, no such expectation can be realized. To be selfish is spiritual death. To think only or chiefly of what concerns only ourselves and our own well-being, temporally or spiritually, is the way of poverty, spiritual destitution, drought and barrenness in all the springs and sources of life. "He that saveth his life shall lose it."

It is the custom and law of the Church that offerings be made for various missionary and charitable objects. A healthful condition of spiritual life depends upon a glad and generous compliance. Your own experience is wide enough to infer with certainty that habitual neglect of meeting such demands brings on a state of deadness which will imperil the prosperity and kill the life of the Parish. The congregational demands that were made the excuse for neglect of Diocesan and general requirements, after a time will not themselves be met, because interest dies out. Indifference, deadness, failure is everywhere.

There is no congregation, whether of Mission or Parish, in which the minimum number of offerings for outside objects should be less than once a month. And for these there ought to be an organized system of solicitation and pledges to be redeemed. It is a sure conclusion from a wide deduction from facts, that it is for the best interests of every congregation as such, to perform this duty with whole-souled generosity and large-heartedness. To do so will bring life into the congregation, and the practical realization of the corporate nature of Christianity, which will intensify all parochial activities, while to neglect it habitually will surely bring on barrenness, torpor and death. The law that determines such result is irreversible.

So much was needful to be said as to the proofs of interest and the practical manner in which those who can do little by personal work may and must show it, and thus follow in spirit the example before us.

The poor restored demoniac was told to go and publish Christ as his Saviour in his own home. He did so, but also beyond. Charity begins at home, but is not circumscribed and does not remain there.

Here is your home. What can you do here? You can do much. Would that you all might open your eyes to see what you might do. You ought to form such Mission districts as are needed in and around your Parish Church. You ought to have half a score or a score of men who would, under appointment as Readers, hold cottage services in as many populous neighborhoods, securing such Clerical supervision and help as may be possible. You ought to have Christian men as well as women organized for such work, banded together for its accomplishment, going out into the highways, inviting all to the Church and to the Missions, and telling all of Jesus the Saviour. You ought to make your Parish or Mission felt as a power for good in every street, in every suburb, in every outside hamlet within your reach. You ought to

make the influence of your Church so potent and so beneficial, that indifference should be attracted, deadness revived, and infidelity itself abashed and silenced.   Men and
women of every class from all around you, from all your
populous streets and outlying districts, as the result of
your efforts, should arise and say, "We will go with you,
for we have heard that the Lord is with you."   So should
the Gospel spread from ten thousand centers and "the
knowledge of the Lord cover the earth as the waters cover
the sea."   Who can for a moment doubt that if such were
the earnest purpose of all our people, if we were determined upon it, would give and work and sacrifice ourselves
for it as is the bounden duty of every Christian, such
glorious results would follow in due time.   Awake, then, to
your duty and your privileges.   Make your lives Christian.   Give yourselves with real interest to your Lord's
work.   Spread abroad a Christian influence.   Build up
your Church, extend it far and wide, and thus array yourselves on the side of Christ and those saved through Him.

XII.

YOUNG MEN AND THEIR WORK IN THE CHURCH.

1 John ii, 14: I write unto you, young men, because
ye are strong and the Word of God abideth in you, and
ye have overcome the wicked one.

IT is the Apostle of love who thus writes. It is near
the close of his life and of the first century, long after
all his brother Apostles had departed. Love, as always, is
his great theme, the love of God manifested in Jesus
Christ, love one towards another. Love prompts his loving instruction to the Churches. He thinks of all. He
has a word for all—the fathers, the young men, even the
little children of the Church. Those little ones had received remission of sins in their baptism, and were therefore responsible for growth in Christ and in the knowledge
of God, which was thereby rendered possible. Fathers
were responsible for the use of their gifts, their knowledge
and experience, their maturity of life and character, in
the service of the Church. Young men were to be strong
in grace as by nature, by the Word of God abiding in them
for overcoming the wicked one, for resisting evil, in behalf
of the Kingdom of Christ.

I propose to take this thought of the strength of young

men as a basis for some remarks upon the work which ought now to be expected of the young men of this (Cathedral) congregation and of the other congregations of our Church in this city. Others besides young men, older men and fathers, and the women of the Church may take useful hints from the suggestions to be offered.

The glory of young men, says Solomon, is their strength. This attributing of strength to young men is very suggestive. They are full of life, activity, energy, enthusiasm. They have a keen pleasure in exertion. They delight in manly effort. Their most pleasant recreation is in physical exercise and feats of agility. They know no fatigue nor weariness when their interest is thoroughly enlisted, in efforts that would be to men of middle life laborious and exhausting.

So always the labors of love are a delight.

But it is spiritual strength rather than physical that the Apostle has in view. He thinks of them as strong in the Lord. They have received the strength of grace in their regeneration and in the covenant of grace. The energy that comes from the spirit of strength and grace is within them and actuates them. They are supposed to have grown in this grace, to have been *confirmed* in it, and had it confirmed in them by the sign and seal of its increase. They are supposed to be carrying their natural earnestness and enthusiasm into their spiritual life ; having renounced the world, to be fighting against the world, and standing in and maintaining that renunciation; to be putting into use their spiritual armour in earnest warfare against sin, making the Word of God in their hands the sword of the Spirit, and wielding it with power, as good soldiers of Jesus Christ.

It is the well-known practice of the sacred writers to speak of the baptized as Christians, as regenerate, enlightened, and to use language of all members of the Church which is strictly applicable only to the spiritually minded, who are walking worthy of their vocation. Some may be very far from the life and character required of them. Still they are in the Church. They are not excommunicate. Therefore they are, by a charitable judgment, presumed to be in heart what they are in rights and privileges, members of Christ, the children of God and inheritors of the Kingdom of Heaven. As they are all this in outward relations, so they are assumed to have at least in some measure the inward character and the life of Christian men. So of all the baptized dead; the Church, committing their bodies to the ground, makes no judgment, utters no censure, but uses rather the general language of Christian hope. When S. John says of young men that they are strong and have the Word of God abiding in them and have overcome the wicked one, he presumes of all the young men in the Church what is true in the fullest measure of but few of them. In all of them it is, he trusts, coming to be true. This is his hope and expectation. They have the Christian vocation. They must not be false to it. They must do their utmost to fulfil it. The germs of the Christian life, the beginnings of the Christian character are in them. In the relations in which they stand, in the vows which are upon them, in the grace and privileges of their membership of Christ, they are strong. The Word of God abideth in them. In potency they have overcome the wicked one, whom they have once for all renounced.

And therefore I cannot be in error if I use S. John's language of the young men in the Church to-day, and say to them all indiscriminately "I speak unto you, young men, because ye are strong and the Word of God abideth in you, and ye have overcome the wicked one." I may assume that you are all, in some sense, what you ought to be, what your position and relations in the Church require of you, what you desire and, it is to be hoped, are striving to be, through the grace of God given and pledged and always sufficient for you.

The Apostle clearly expects much of young men in the Church. They have large capabilities. The Church has a just claim upon their natural endowments, their earnestness and activity. They ought to be in the fore-front of every active movement, the advance guard, and the strong arm in every battle of the Church. They are to stand shoulder to shoulder in serried ranks, irresistible in their strength, as they go forth in warfare against the Church's enemies.

He addresses the young men as a class. In other cases where classes of persons are spoken of in regard to any office or work in the Church, co-operation, associated effort is implied. So of the Ministry, whether of Apostles, Elders or Deacons. So of women, deaconesses, widows, under the direction of the Apostles or other Ministers. Of little children it is implied that they are associated in learning, in receiving a training in grace by the Word of God; of fathers, as especially bound together in love, in tastes, habits and duties. Young men are classed together as being strong, as being engaged in work in which their strength is available. Hence we may regard them as mutually co-operating and organizing their work, which is the overcoming of the wicked one and the sin and misery of the world around them.

Indeed, the principle of organization is fundamental in Christianity. It is involved in membership of Christ. All the members have their functions, and co-operate to the perfecting of the Body. It is seen in worship which is common, united, social. It is seen in the work of the Ministry and of all who labor in the cause of Christ. Christianity is indeed in its very nature corporate. It is embodied in an organism, an institution, the Church of God. All work that is effective is organized. The world has derived from the Church the principle of association for the accomplishment of results, and it is made the chief instrument of progress and of civilization, and everybody knows how combination, co-operation, is the secret of large successes in all worldly enterprise. It involves division of labor, grades of office and of functions, some supplying what others lack, and all uniting in different ways, by divers means and methods, in the bringing about of great ends.

It is the carrying out of the same principle which is implied in the Lord's choosing the College of the Apostles and the Presbyterate of the Seventy; in the employment of the young men as assistants to the Ministry, as seen in the fifth chapter of the Acts; in the appointment of the seven Deacons; in the associate missionary work of the Apostles and Evangelists; in the Conciliar action of the Apostles and Elders and brethren. I insist, therefore, upon this as a legitimate inference, that the young men of the Church must be looked to as a class in associated action for the doing of work in which they have special qualifications. I write unto you, young men, because ye are strong. I claim in behalf of the Church the use of that strength which God has given you, in the service of the Church and the Gospel of Jesus Christ.

The idea of an association of young men for Christian work in the Church is a grand and noble one, and ought to be realized in all our large parishes. In cities like this, it should be formed of all the young men willing to engage in active Church work, in all the Parishes and Missions. Ultimately there would be a Diocesan association formed of all the local associations in the several cities and towns. Many of the English Dioceses have their lay helpers' associations of men who have already done great things for the Church. By visitors, readers and teachers, the Gospel has been brought home to many souls. Districts that had been abandoned to heathenism have been reclaimed, purified, enlightened, civilized. In this country at least one Diocese, that of Long Island, has its lay helpers' association admirably organized and doing most effective work for the Church, in its missions to the poor and working people, and in the administration of its charities.

Let us see what the idea is. No principle can be more obvious, whether in the light of Holy Scripture or in the experience of Christian history than this: that every Christian association, whether of men or women, whatever its objects, to be wise and safe and largely beneficial in relation to Christianity, must be in the Church, under its authority, and a part of its living organism. There must be no self-will in it. It must be loyal to the Church, its doctrine, discipline and usages. Love, obedience, hearty co-operation, thorough devotion are essential. Whether there be preaching and exhortation, or Mission services and Sunday-schools with district visiting, whatever it be that is undertaken, it must be under authority and strict accountability. The association, to be permanently Chris-

tian and justify its name, must be in the Church, in subor-
dination to the officers of the Church, actuated by the
Church's spirit and principles, an ally of the Church's
Ministry.

Other associations may be needful and useful for other
purposes. I am not questioning the legitimacy of scientific associations, musical or art associations, lectureship
and literary associations. These and other like associations may claim the membership and receive the aid of
Christians, for not all secular things are evil. It is altogether another kind of association I am advocating: one
that is Christian, the very idea of which involves its being
in the Church, the very object of which is to do some portion of the Church's work in alliance with and in sub-
ordination to the Church's Ministry, and under her laws
and government.

The work which the Church is set to do imperatively
requires such an Association, and cannot well be done without it. The work is pressing. It must be done. Failure
to do it will be fatal.

The Church needs the strength of young men. The
Church believes in them, yearns for them, loves them.
She would marshal them into combined and effective ac-
tion in her glorious work of breaking down the kingdom
of sin, Satan and death, and extending the Kingdom of our
Redeemer.

What we want here is a young men's association, or

brotherhood, for charitable and missionary work. It should be organized in connection with the Cathedral, but each parish should have its chapter, all united in the central organization on equal terms. Its work should be to establish and conduct Missions, Mission Sunday-schools, cottage lectures, and to aid the hospital and charitable work; to secure subscriptions, friends, helpers, in aid of the parochial and other authorities in charge. There will be various committees for different departments of effort. Some will superintend schools. Some will be teachers. Some will be lay readers. Some will be visitors. Some will look after the sick and afflicted. Some will secure funds for designated objects. Some will visit families, and seek out the children and indigent and uncared-for people for whom the Church is responsible. All will seek out strangers, and especially young men, bring them to Church and make them feel at home; gather them into Bible classes, enlist their interest in the Missions, and by every means convince all such people as are yet outside the influences of Christianity that the Church is their home and their best friend; its teaching and spiritual helps what their souls need; its work worthy of their strength and labor; its society and associations elevating, helpful, enjoyable.

Thus young men associated together, and organized, and strong in the Lord, might make grand use of their strength in His service. They might carry the Gospel

and the Kingdom of Christ into all the waste places
around us, scattering the darkness with the light of truth
and opening the door of hope and salvation to multitudes
of perishing souls.

The association should have its regular meetings, at
which the Bishop, Dean or one or more of the Clergy should
be present, for reports, for consultation, for maturing plans
of action. Besides the missionary objects, there might be
the further one of social pleasure, mutual improvement or
Christian edification. There might be the reading-room,
the library, the courses of lectures, the classes of instruction, affording facilities to acquire the knowledge requisite
for any branch of business or mechanical or scientific pur-
suit. There might be debates, readings, dissertations.
All this, however, should be subsidiary to the great work
in which strength, zeal, earnestness are necessary: the
overcoming of the wicked one in all his wiles, the saving of
souls from his dominion and gathering them into the fold
of Christ. The St. Andrew's Brotherhood, with its branch
in each parish and its general chapter of the city and,
in due time, of the Diocese, with its twofold promise and
vow for its members that each shall endeavor to bring at
least one man every Sunday to the Church or to the Bible
class and to pray for the extension of Christ's kingdom
among men, might enlarge the scope of its work and
answer all the purposes necessary. It is an admirable organization. Its plan deserves the heartiest commendation.

It should be introduced into every Parish. It bids fair to become the right arm of the Church in her missionary work among the classes of people from whom should come her most promising recruits and whom she has hitherto culpably neglected ;—I mean the workingmen, the bone and sinew of the country.

Glorious will be the day for the Church (in Denver) when our young men, of whom there are so many, strong to labor, shall unite in all such work as now invites their co-operation. Long have we waited and prayed for the time when this great movement might be inaugurated under such favorable auspices as to promise success. How much of the strength of young men have I seen wasted, lost to the Church, lost to their own souls. How much of it goes to the world and its pursuits, its vain and futile pleasures and their exactions, to yield to which is unmanly and slavish.

Rejoice, O young man, in thy youth, and let thy heart cheer thee in the days of thy youth, but remember that if your enjoyment is sought and found only in this world, a day of drear and bitter sorrow will surely follow your joy. Rejoice in your strength, but not in using it at the behests of the wicked one, or of the world, or of self. Rejoice to use it for Christ. It comes from God ; it must be consecrated to God. If given to the wicked one it will be a curse. It will make your ruin sure and irremediable. The best, the most noble, the most manly work you can do with the strength, natural and spiritual, God gives you, is what you may do for Him, for the Church, for the souls and bodies of men. The most effective work you can do is as united and in co-operation. Set it before you, then, as an object to be speedily attained, to undertake, in association and as a brotherhood, the strong, aggressive missionary work of saving souls, of improving the intellectual, moral, spiritual condition of men, of sustaining the missions, the schools, the hospital, the charities of the Church, and whatsoever else there may be for you to do for Christ. Determine that all shall be done with earnest Christian purpose in the spirit of love, loyalty and obedience, and willing sacrifice for Christ's sake. And let us ask His blessing upon whatever may be done to His glory, the extension of His Church and kingdom, and the salvation of souls.

XIII.

WOMAN'S WORK IN THE CHURCH.

Romans xvi, 12: Salute Tryphena and Tryphosa who labor in the Lord. Salute the beloved Persis which labored much in the Lord.

WE hear much in these days about woman's rights. It is time to begin the discussion of woman's duties. It is only in exceptional cases in this country that the rights of all classes are not guaranteed and secured. It is not uncommon to find both individuals and classes neglecting imperative duties. The most effectual way to obtain our rights is to fulfil all our obligations. And the consequence of neglecting duties is the forfeiture of rights. These principles are not peculiar in their application, either to men or women.

The Church of Christ has elevated woman to a high sphere of duty and responsibility, and has thus restored to her her rights. That her social position in Christian lands is not what it has been, and still is, in heathen countries, is due, without question, to the religion of Jesus Christ. So far as she had any ministry in connection with religion among the heathen, it was one that only served to degrade her. We make only this very moderate statement,

186

without further reference to the abominations attendant upon the services of women in the Temples of ancient Idolatry.

In the Jewish dispensation, her membership of the Church, though recognized as real, was rather involved in that of men, than conferred expressly and independently. Still women were treated with gentleness and often with reverence; and many among them attained to the highest eminence by their talents and piety. But it was reserved for Christianity to exalt woman to the high rank she now enjoys in the Church and in society. Our Lord found among women the most ardent and faithful disciples, and the most efficient in ministering to His wants. The Son of God, in becoming Incarnate, was born of a woman. Thus was conferred upon womanhood the highest honor and a transcendent glory. She whom all men should call blessed,—she who was so highly favored, is properly the type of what woman in Christ should seek to become. No privilege could be greater than to belong to that sex, upon which the Mother of our Lord and God conferred such distinction. Observe the confidence our Lord reposed in women and the fidelity of their ministrations. The names of the Marys and others are as imperishable as those of the Apostles. As often remarked, holy women were "last at the Cross and first at the Sepulchre" on Easter morning. Holy women were part of the Church which waited for the promise of the Father, the coming of the Holy Ghost,

the Comforter. The gifts of the Spirit descended upon
women, and not upon men only. They equally shared in
the Church's Baptism and Eucharistic Feast. They were
ministered unto, and themselves fulfilled a ministry. It
was the widows of the Helenistic portion of the Church
at Jerusalem, that gave occasion to the appointment of the
Seven Deacons. And that there were Deaconesses in the
Apostolic Church is scarcely more doubtful than that
there were Deacons. S. Paul says, writing to the Romans,
" I commend unto you Phebe, our Sister, which is a servant
(Greek, a *Deaconess*) of the Church which is at Cenchrea."
She was evidently a person of much consideration. S.
Paul recommends her at greater length than any others;
" that ye receive her in the Lord as becometh Saints, and
that ye assist her in whatsoever business she hath need of
you, for she hath been a succourer of many and of me
also." In S. Paul's first Epistle to Timothy a literal
translation of the Greek would seem to show, and in this
agree the best ancient and modern interpreters—that
where we read of the wives of Deacons, the meaning
is really, *female Deacons.* "Even so must the women
Deaconesses be grave, not slanderers, sober, faithful in all
things." As in the Gospels, the Marys, Joannas, Susannas,
ministered unto the Lord of their substance, so in the
Acts, the example is followed by godly women, like
Dorcas, who was "full of good works and also of alms
deeds which she did;" and Priscilla, the wife of Aquila

the Jew of Pontus, who assisted her husband in expounding the way of God more perfectly to Apollos, the eloquent teacher of the Corinthians. There was also a recognized class of widows, and somewhat later, of virgins, who had their regular functions and duties, and received, as such, the support of the faithful.

That Deaconesses were an Order in the Post Apostolic Church is proved by abundant witnesses. Pliny the younger, Governor of Bythinia, writing to the Emperor Trajan, at the beginning of the second century, speaks of two Deaconesses of whom he sought to prove, by torture, the truth concerning those strange confessions of the Christians: "that they were wont on a stated day to meet before the dawn, and repeat among themselves, in alternate measure, a hymn to Christ as God, and by their vow to bind themselves, not to the committing of any crime, but against theft and robbery and adultery, and breach of faith and denial of trust, after which it was their custom to depart and again to meet for the purpose of taking food,"—probably to celebrate the Lord's Supper. The Apostolic Constitutions which are evidence of the customs of the Church from the latter part of the third century, recognize the female Diaconate, as do S. Chrysostom and other Fathers at a later period. Many Deaconesses are mentioned by name and their successful labors in the conversion of souls specially commemorated.*

*On this whole subject, see Bingham's Antiquities of the Christian Church. Also the useful little work of Mr. Ludlow, on "Woman's Work in the Church."

But it is not our purpose to pursue this subject into patristic history, nor to show the position of Deaconesses, widows, sisters, or virgins in the several periods of the Church. Our object is rather to notice some of the hints the writers of the New Testament give us, of woman's work in the Church, and to point out the work and ministry she is now called upon to enter, and some of the modes in which she may discharge it.

Some evidence that an Order of Deaconesses existed in the Apostolic Church has been presented, and also that there was a class of widows with a recognized ministry in the service of God. The fact warrants an inference of the highest importance. As the ministry of Apostle-Bishops, Priests and Deacons did not exclude the active work of all the brethren, but, on the contrary, supposed and required it, so the female Diaconate was not the " exceptional monopoly of woman's work and functions." After Phebe, the Deaconess, S. Paul makes mention of " Mary, who bestowed much labor on us ;" of " Tryphena and Tryphosa, who labor in the Lord," and " the beloved Persis, who labored much in the Lord ;" and in another Epistle, of " those women who labored with me in the Gospel." Nor is it said that Dorcas or Priscilla were Deaconesses. All these faithful women probably did the work which was equally the duty and privilege of all the women in the Church of Christ.

It is evident from these brief Scripture references that

women have a most important sphere and work in the Church. It is also clear that, if Apostolic precedent is to have any weight ; if, what the Apostles instituted or sanctioned, guided as they were by the Lord's instructions and the inspiration of the Holy Spirit in their action as well as in their teaching, is to be followed implicitly as the law for all after ages—a vital principle in all Churches of Apostolic foundation and a Catholic history—there should be in every age and in every part of the Church regularly appointed Deaconesses or Sisters, for the same work for which such an Order was originally found necessary ; just as was undoubtedly the case for several centuries, before the extravagant notion of an inherent superiority in a life of virginity gave rise to the supposed angelic life, espousal to Christ, and nuns and nunneries, enforced vows, and all the abuses of female monasticism.

The attempted restoration of this Order in the reformed Catholic Church is more than justified. Indeed, this is the imperative duty of every branch of the Church, which claims the Bible as interpreted by the Church in the past ages, as its rule of faith and practice. And the success of every effort in this direction is only what might be expected. The inference cannot be set aside, that it is the will of Christ that His Church should be served by the ministry of Deaconesses or Sisters, as well as of Deacons and other Orders. And now that the work which the Church is called to do is pressing upon us, and we are waking up to a sense of its magnitude and of the need of more laborers, and the faithful are everywhere searching for the best instrumentalities and methods, by the study of Holy Scripture and the example of the primitive ages of Faith and of most successful labor, there can hardly be a doubt that we shall soon have the primitive Diaconate revived and restored among us ; we shall have Deaconesses under this or some other name, as that of Sisters, success-fully laboring in every Parish, in the schools of the Church, and in hospitals, homes and asylums, for all classes of the afflicted. We shall have teaching Deaconesses or Sisters for our Parish schools, which will by and by be seen to be necessary, not for a salary, but with the assurance of the Church's support and care through life. We shall have Deaconesses or Sisters regularly employed in winning to Christ both men and women, and imparting primary instruction, and ministering to the sick and needy under the care and maintenance of the Church. The sanction given to this office and work of women in the Church of England, and by the General Convention of the American Church, is one of the most hopeful of the signs of the times. It gives us hope that the thorough working out of a principle of the Gospel so generally recognized, cannot be long delayed.

But our Scripture data would not be fully satisfied even with such results. Besides the Deaconesses, " grave, not slanderers, sober, faithful in all things;" besides those,

like " Phebe, the Deaconess which is of the Church at
Cenchrea," there must be many laborers in the Lord,
and helpers to the ministry, like Tryphena and Tryphosa,
and the beloved Persis ; like the holy women whose gentle ministries cheered the life of the Lord on earth ; like
Dorcas, "full of good works and alms deeds;" like Priscilla, who could assist in expounding the Scriptures in
the rich fullness of their meaning to those less perfectly
instructed. As all men are pledged to a personal work
for Christ when they are sealed with the sign of the Cross,
and when the Holy Ghost is given in the laying on of
hands, so must the same responsibilities be realized by
women in general, in the Christian community. There
must be no drones in the hive. There must be no idle
hangers-on about the Christian camp, no useless members
of the Body.

Indeed, the examples we have cited, and the plain teaching of the Apostles, justifies the employment of the services
of Christian women in any and every way in which experience has found or may find it available, as Sisters of Mercy,
nursing the sick, caring for the poor, winning the neglected
to the Church of Christ, teaching in schools, conducting
men's Bible classes and mothers' meetings, Bible reading,
tract distribution and parochial visitation.   There is every
reason derived from Scripture and from experience, why all
women in the Church should engage in these good works,
so far as they have time and opportunity.   There is every

reason why those who are qualified, or by training can acquire the qualifications, and who are not hindered by family ties or other necessary duties, should devote themselves to such works of love and mercy for definite periods under the support and guidance of the Church. Surely we must not yield to a vulgar and unreasoning prejudice against the work which is required by the binding and perpetual vow of Christian profession. If the Christian woman, anxious to serve her Lord in His Church, finds that she can give a day each week to His exclusive work without neglect of the duties of her state of life, why may she not pledge this to Him in a fixed resolve for such time as her circumstances shall remain the same? If she is free from home cares and duties, so that for any period she would feel justified in an engagement for teaching or secular labor, why may she not, with equal safety, pledge to the Church her services for the same time under like conditions? It is an absurd prejudice, foolish beyond measure and to the last degree harmful, that would restrain a woman from a pledge of work for Christ on stated days, or for a stated time, longer or shorter, under the express condition of a release of the obligation, should any providential change of circumstances make such release desirable. The catholic work of the Church cannot be done as it ought, without the aid of women; for history and experience show that without such aid it never was done fully. And this work must not be spasmodic. It must be given as we give ourselves to Christ, ungrudgingly and without reserve. It must be so given that it can be relied on, and organized into practical efficiency.

We must add a word on the social influence of women in the Church, which is absolutely necessary to the success of a Parish. If the Communion of Saints is to be more than a doctrine of the Creed; if it is to be realized practically, so far as it relates to the members of the Church militant in their mutual relations, in social intercourse, in the fellowship of all classes who are brought together and made one in Christ, the ministry of godly women will be found essential. What would society be without the gentle, refining, elevating influence of woman? The Church is a society. Its worship is social. All within it stand in intimate social relations. All should be interested in one another. All are to be mutually helpful. The privileges and blessings of the Gospel are to be enjoyed in common. Not only in public worship, but in frequent meetings for social intercourse, for promoting mutual acquaintance, for healthful recreations and social pleasures of a refining and elevating character, should all the members of a Parish be brought together for the development and exercise of the social instincts and sympathies which the Creator has implanted, and which are essential to a vigorous and healthful Church life. But what would be the value of such assemblies and such intercourse without the presence and influence of woman, formed and endowed, as she is by nature, to be the mistress of society, to give guidance, tone and character to social intercourse? Here, then, there is a department of work in which the cause of Christ may be served in a manner the most effectual, in which all good women may have a share.

We conclude with the obvious remark, that if all women in the Church would but renounce "the pomps and vanities" of the world, the engrossments of dress and fashion, and the absorbing pleasures of those who are dead while they live; if they would but leave all to follow Christ, according to their vow, and realize their relations to all who are in Christ and all for whom He died, especially the poor, the careless and uncared for, the hardened and the wretched; and if they would let their love for Christ become an active principle constraining their efforts, and would minister to men as a service to Himself: what hard impenitence is there that they might not soften, what coldness and indifference that they might not dispel, what sorrows that they might not soothe, and sufferings alleviate, and thereby win the objects of their interest to faith, and love, and truth, and duty, by their unselfishness, their tender sympathy, and their love and devotion; making them respectable, because respecting themselves, and putting them in the way of honor among men, and of the higher dignity of a position of usefulness in the Church of God. If all women would but begin to enter upon their " vocation and ministry " as Christians, and would thus learn the power for good with which they are intrusted, instead of prating about their rights, which no right-minded person disputes, how would they not become ennobled in character and exalted in position, and how surely would the way be opened for all the organized services of women which the Church so imperatively requires. It is a cause of thankfulness that there are so many who realize their mission. May their number speedily increase !

XIV.

1 Peter iv, 11: If any man minister let him do it as
of the ability which God giveth, that God in all things
may be glorified through Jesus Christ.

THE question has been much agitated of late years,
"What is the best mode of working a Parish?"
The discussion of this question has led to many valuable
suggestions, which have been practically tested with a good
measure of success, by some of our more advanced clergy
and parishes. We use the word "advanced" in its obvious
and true sense, as applying to those who are striving to get
out of the old ruts and the beaten ways of Church work,
and to adopt more efficient methods. The result has been
—and we are seeing it more and more—the abandonment
by those "who have understanding of the times to know
what Israel ought to do," of the grand ideal of the good
Parish which was almost universal till within a few years :
that their work for Christ was sufficiently well done by
minister and people, if the church was open for those who
chose to come on Sundays and perhaps once in the week,
and who paid pew rents ; if the service was according to
the standard of sober and dull monotony, of prayers
198

preached to the people, of quartette singing in which no voice of the congregation could join, of subdued and whispered responses and AMENS unuttered with the lips, of formal, prosy, orthodox preaching, and general self-satisfaction with the observance of the proprieties of a Sunday worship; if the minister could find time, beyond what was required for the usual tea-drinking and social visiting among the better classes, to make a formal call once or twice in a year upon all the families under his care, with proper attention to the sick and the dispensation of the alms of the Church to the few poor and needy; if the sewing society was kept busy in preparing for fairs as often as they were needed, and the vestry, with such help, succeeded in keeping the Parish respectably self-supporting. But with the gradual disappearance of this well-known type of parochial life, the number of the worldly, selfish, and self-indulgent Clergy, who thought themselves painfully laborious, has greatly diminished, and the brethren of the laity have found that they have a "vocation and ministry" in co-operation with the Clergy in the work of the Parish. Now that it is seen and generally admitted that the instrumentalities hitherto employed to Christianize our own country have to a large extent failed, and that consequently less than a third of the people anywhere attend public worship of any kind, even on Sundays; and fully half of our population, both in city and country, are in a condition of practical heathenism as regards the knowledge and the practice of the Gospel of Jesus Christ, it is beginning also to be felt that the opportunity of this Church has come; that we must prove the Apostolicity and catholicity of our claims, not so much by writing apologies, as by Apostolic and catholic labors; that instead of being content to minister to a small aristocratic and cultivated class, we must aim directly to reach the masses; that we must popularize our services, and make them warm, earnest, and attractive to all sorts and conditions of men; that we must begin to lay large foundations of education and charity, and develop all our resources in carrying the Gospel in the Church—and not as a sentiment, nor as a system of speculative opinions—home to every man, and make it felt as the power of God unto salvation, to poor as well as rich, ignorant as well as learned, rude and uncultivated as well as elegant and refined. If we are to do this, it is obvious that we must get all our forces into healthy action, and bring into exercise instrumentalities and modes of work of which the primitive Church affords abundant examples, but which have been until recently almost unknown and untried among us.

In the attempts that have been made to set forth better modes of parochial working, the great object to be kept in view has not been sufficiently regarded. That object is to bring to practical acceptance, and realization, the Christianity which the Church presents among all those classes of our population who are living without any true recognition of Christ and of His claims upon their hearts and lives; and thus to bring ALL the people into living and active relations with Christ in and through His Body the Church, and hearty, enthusiastic co-operation in carrying the same Gospel, embodied in Christ's own Institution, throughout the whole world. Subsidiary to this great end are all the means for the care of the bodies as well as the souls of men: the organization of charities for greater effect, as well as to prevent the abuses of thoughtless and spasmodic almsgiving, such as the increase of pauperism and systematic beggary; for the establishment and fostering of sound institutions of learning; schools of training for teachers and workers in every sphere in which the Church needs regular helpers, working with system and under authority; and institutions for the support and maintenance of those who in any capacity give their lives exclusively to the Church's service; for securing the free and liberal gifts of all the faithful, according to the Gospel measure of proportion to the gifts and blessings received; and leading all the members of the Church up to that standard of Christian living in which there shall be "no place left for error in religion or for viciousness of life." No object less exalted and thorough than this can lead to the most satisfactory results.

The first and indispensable requisite in parochial work is the Rector, who is by his office the head of the Parish. Though Parishes may be and often are the result of lay effort with only occasional clerical assistance and oversight, yet generally in established Parishes no more can be done without the Rector than in the army without the commander. The proverb is true, " Like priest like people." Our observation has convinced us that the poor results of most of our old parochial organizations are chiefly due to the bad management and inefficiency of the Clergy in charge. Whose fault, but theirs, can it be that so many Parishes fail to give the practical support of offerings to the great missionary cause of the Church in its several departments, the carrying on of which with efficiency is essential to the Church's life, thus depriving their people of that important means of blessing, and putting them in a position of apparent disloyalty to Christ Himself?

Our clerical brethren will pardon us if we point out some of the most necessary though least often inculcated of the Rector's qualifications for success as a Parish priest, on the assumption, which will not be questioned, that success will depend in a great measure on his ability to enlist the earnest and harmonious co-operation of all the people.

We take it for granted that he is to be a man of prayer and devout holy life ; that he is to be thoroughly conversant with Holy Scripture, and sound theology, and good learning ; and qualified to meet the doubts of the people, which are insinuated in the multifarious secular literature of the day, as well as by books of more pretentious character upon science and philosophy. He ought to be a man able to command respect for weight of character and solid acquirements. Even as a man, he must let no man despise him.

But he must be above all things a minister of Jesus Christ. He must have a full consciousness of what was meant when it was said to him, "receive the Holy Ghost," or "take thou authority," in his ordination to the priesthood. He must feel that a gift of God is in him by the laying on of hands, to be stirred up by constant prayer and effort. He must magnify his office, not by word only, but by deed ; not by arrogant claims, but by arduous and unremitting labors in humble, self-denying ministries in the name and for the sake of his Lord and Master. He must beseech men, *in Christ's stead,* to be reconciled to God. He must fulfil his public duties in the Church, as one who realizes that he is a Minister of Christ and a steward of the mysteries of God. In his visitations among the people, whether the sick or the whole, he must not go merely as a friend, with the ordinary sympathy which every Christian heart must feel for ignorance, spiritual insensibility, and physical or mental suffering. He must go officially ; he must go as sent, in the fulfilment of functions divinely given. Such a consciousness of ministerial character will give him confidence and courage. When he thinks of himself, he will say, " Who is sufficient for these things?" But when he considers that he is the representative of Christ Himself, he will say, " I can do all things through Christ strengthening me."

This constant realization of his ministerial character is necessary to his influence. It will insure obedience to his counsels. It will enable him to get work done. It belongs to human nature to recognize legitimate authority. So strong is this tendency that people do not always stop to ascertain whether it be legitimate. They recognize it as claimed. A man born to command may, with a firm will, a steady eye, and the voice of authority, rule and control the mob. He who is qualified both by nature and office will, like the centurion, "say to one, Go, and he goeth; and to another, Come, and he cometh."

We are well aware how surely the Rector will frustrate his own endeavors and defeat his ends by the appearance of undue self-confidence, and an overbearing disposition and self-complacency of manner, as well as by lack of good sense and sound judgment and discretion. He must be really humble and self-distrustful, and he will be so regarded. At the same time he must act habitually upon his commission. He must assume the functions he is sent to fulfil. He must be in all things Christ's Minister, not as one self-appointed and self-qualified, but empowered for his work with all needed grace, that he may go forth humbly, and yet boldly and courageously, to all the duties of his ministry. Then he will inspire confidence. His own single-heartedness, and earnestness, and enthusiasm will attract and inspire others ; and when they are led to see the work to be done and to feel their own responsibility, he will be able to set them in ways of Christian activity and usefulness.

Some Clergymen are apparently very earnest and inde-fatigable in labors, and yet they lack in effectiveness. They are constantly busied in hurrying from place to place, visiting, preaching, becoming acquainted with every-body, giving kind words, and doing many things which are not so necessary, and which others might do as well ; but yet their work does not tell ; they see no permanent results. It is but a tread-mill sort of labor, or moving about in a circle, as the progress of their thought is apt to be in preaching. Thus they spend much of their strength for naught.

He is but a poor captain who undertakes to do the work of his under officers and his privates. The Rector should never do himself what he can legitimately put upon others.

We spoke of the great end, with its subordinate parts, which every Rector should have in view. We believe that it is necessary, in order that all that is done in parochial work may help in the promotion of the end of the increased godliness and of the growth of the Parish and of the growth of the Church, that the Rector should have a plan or policy to be steadily held and consistently acted on in all things. It should not be formed suddenly. It must be the result of mature reflection, in view of all the conditions. He may grow up to it. It may take shape gradually in his mind. But without it, his success can only be partial and temporary.

Of course, we can only speak of it in general terms, because it will differ as the conditions and circumstances differ in which Parish work is to be done. It is sufficient to say that it must be broad, comprehensive, embracing all that needs to be accomplished, and looking far into the future. It must have many subordinate parts, but all its details must be such as to subserve the great end, the building up of the kingdom of Christ in all human hearts, and as a visible institution which shall be able to bring Christ's redemption of soul and body, in every sense in which He came to redeem us, to all whom the blessed Gospel can reach.

But this plan or policy must not be talked about. The Rector must not tell beforehand what he is going to do, if it is of an unusual character. Many a Minister has brought defeat upon some wise and noble purpose by disclosing it prematurely and exciting opposition and violent dissensions. The Clergy, much more than other men, must learn to keep secrets, their own as well as those of other people. They must also learn to be patient and to wait. What cannot be done now may be by and by. What cannot be done in one way, or by one class of instruments, may still be possible in other ways or by other means. The Rector is required to prepare the way of the Lord. He must create, or choose and mould his own instruments. He must bring about the emergencies for which his plan is to provide.

He will open his plan little by little; first, in some of its subordinate details, to those in whose co-operation he relies. Their sympathy with him in these will qualify them for further disclosures and fuller confidence. Some will be set at one part of the work; some at another, as they show the needed qualifications. They will be fully instructed, each in his own work and its nature and purpose, so as to be able to do it well. But it may be all preparatory to something more and higher, which the workers will at the proper time be prepared to see, which will perhaps suggest itself to them as necessary, and will secure their earnest and efficient aid. They will often take up, as their own, lines of action to which the Rector's instruction has led them. Thus he works with their hands. This is always most encouraging.

Suppose it were in the Rector's plan to establish a cottage hospital, as it might be and probably should be in most large Parishes, except in the great cities, where the workers in the several Parishes should combine in one general effort of larger character and upon a grander scale. To speak of his purpose at the first would frighten people in rural

Parishes. Hence, he instructs his congregation by preaching and pastoral intercourse in their duty in relation to the aged, and the sick, and homeless. He awakens their sympathies in behalf of the classes of sufferers for whom he would have them provide. After such preparation, two or three persons will be found to visit and report such persons as require assistance. As many others can be secured to spend a certain portion of time, pledged beforehand if possible, in reading to sick, or aged, or other disabled people at their homes. By and by they will venture, after reading and instruction, to kneel for prayer. Others will collect hospital stores for distribution as needed. In due time a family may be found, the lady of which will be willing to receive an occasional homeless person who needs food and shelter, and perhaps others who are sick or helpless. The occasion will thus be made to rent, purchase, or build, and to provide a matron, beds, and all things necessary. And the work will be set in full operation, with increasing income for growing necessities. In this way there will be no place for opposition, and all will be led on in harmony. We give this simply as an illustration. In a like way, from small beginnings, with right direction, permanent agencies, and modes of charity and of education, with brotherhoods and sisterhoods, and schools of training for such as can give themselves wholly to work for Christ may be established, with untold results for good in the future.

No Rector of a Parish can rest satisfied till he has found some work for all his people to do on whom God has not already laid sufficient burdens of care and duty in which to promote His cause. For we should not forget that they who are called to suffer with Christ, who endure afflictions from His hand, in His spirit, and for His sake, and they who are employed in the care and Christian nurture of His children, given by Him and placed under their guidance and training; and even those who serve Him in fervency of spirit by diligence in business, who rightly regard their stewardship of His gifts, are all doing His work, helping to extend His kingdom, and promoting His glory. But there are many in every Parish who have time which God's service has the right to claim, and which otherwise would be given to selfish work or pleasure, or mere sloth and listlessness. There are many ways in which the discreet and efficient Rector can enlist the help of all such members of the Church as are not hindered by duties which are providentially imposed. But an important and necessary caution should be suggested. Young clergymen, in their zeal, often make haste to devise a system of machinery into which to organize as parts all those whose co-operation they hope to secure. The result is that they must themselves supply continually all the motive power, or it ceases working, and becomes disordered and disorganized. They are themselves exhausted in the effort to impart life and movement, and the work accomplished is small. It is, therefore, necessary, first to awaken and to deepen the spiritual life of the people ; to show them and make them feel how much there is to be done, and which, without their assistance, must be neglected ; to impart a deep sense of their own individual responsibility in the Church's work, and of the need that they should stir up and employ all the gifts of God, whether of nature or of grace. When they " have a mind to work," not till then, can their labors be organized effectively. The life must be first, then there will be growth ; and growth is necessarily organic. The life of a Parish, as of the Church at large, will manifest itself in healthful and beneficent organization. The Rector is in a position to cultivate and direct it, so as to make it subserve his ends. His wisdom will be shown in knowing how, and being prompt and timely to give this direction. He must not allow any force to go to waste, or to expend itself destructively. There are many good people whose zeal and energy would seek manifestations of a one-sided and partial character, and in ways destructive of order, harmony, and unity. By care and forethought such persons may be used with good results, if put in the proper place, in work for which they are fitted. It will not do to leave them to themselves. It is not safe to give them time to produce disorder and con-flict. Put them at the work which they like, but rule them with delicacy, with tact, with a firm and strong hand. They are strong-minded, but will yield gracefully to the direction of superior strength and wisdom, combined with rightful authority.

These remarks are for the Clergy as well as the laity. The value they claim is not theoretical. They are the result of experience. They are intended to be only suggestive. A word to the wise is sufficient.

This Church is now feeling a mighty impulse of revival. Not only is she moving forward with rapid strides upon ground hitherto unoccupied ; she is feeling the pulse of a more vigorous life in her members. The very eccentricities of extreme opinions and action are symptoms of a living and not a dead or decaying body. There are better symptoms, especially in the founding of homes and hospitals and sisterhoods, and the organization of lay helpers, and in the efforts put forth with much success at so many points to reach those whom God has not blessed with wealth, the great middle class, from whom will come, in the next or following generation, by right of power, both politically and socially, the rulers of the people.

It becomes all our Clergy and laity to be alive with the life of the Church ; to let it call forth and determine their activities ; to help to increase its mighty volume and power, and thus to have their own part in bringing on the glorious days which are in store—if she is faithful—for this American branch of the Catholic and Apostolic Church.

XV.

S. Luke xi, 17 : Every kingdom divided against
itself is brought to desolation.

OUR Lord announced this general principle for the purpose of putting to silence His enemies. They said
that He cast out devils by Beelzebub. This could not be.
The Prince of the Kingdom of Evil could not lend a part of
his power to be wielded by Him Who came to destroy the
works of the devil. To do this, would be to suffer his
kingdom to be divided against itself, and thus to be
brought to desolation.

There is, then, a Kingdom of the Prince of Evil. If
the powers of wickedness were not organized, they would
have little strength. Evil is essentially depraving, disinte-
grating and anarchical. It cannot create. It can only ruin
and destroy. To do its work, it must be compacted into a
system. It must have a unity, though opposition, antagonism only, can unite discordant elements. It must have its
head, its subordinate officers, its gradations of powers and
functions, working in loyal subjection and harmony for its

212

baneful purposes. Thus the forces of Satan, organized into a kingdom, in combined array and under discipline, confront Christ, and all who are His, and all the good of which He is the author.

The text declares a universal truth. *Every* kingdom divided against itself is brought to desolation. If Christ has a kingdom, if He is really the Head of a kingdom, it must be applicable to this kingdom. There can be no impropriety in using the text as suggestive of the subject of the Kingdom of Christ and the strength it has in the harmonious adjustment of its ruling and working forces, the unity and co-operation of its members.

It was necessary that Christ should have a kingdom, if His religion was to be permanent and successful. There are Christian people, apparently not conversant with Scripture or history, who hold that Christianity, as promulgated by our Lord and His Apostles, had no fixed and definite polity, no regular organization ; that it is only a revelation of Truth, a scheme of remedial agencies, a plan of salvation, and that its essence is in the adoption of this scheme or plan, the belief of its doctrines, and the living of the life which it requires. In other words, Christianity is a doctrinal system, an idea and a life. The idea, it is admitted, tends to take a concrete form. Those who believe will naturally associate themselves together. The forms of organization will be various, according to the preferences of believers, and the exigencies of times and circumstances.

According to this view there is, strictly speaking, no actual Kingdom of Christ among men, no divine polity and government of the Church, no pre-ordained form of the Ministry, no fixed principles of order, legislation and discipline, which were to be the same, essentially, from age to age.

If this had been the nature of Christianity, what would have been its future? How could it have succeeded in the world? It must be evident to thoughtful people, conversant with the conditions of its propagation, that it could not have survived in its integrity the second century. As a system of ideas or doctrines merely, it would have taken the forms of schools of thought, and would have shared the fate of other systems of like character. We can see what would have become of Christianity from what did actually occur. The Oriental mind, embracing parts of the Christian system, sought to mould it into its own forms of thought. The Heathen Philosophies became modified in the process. From the mixture of divine and human elements came forth the strangest systems. The divine Philosophy was corrupted into the most incongruous human theories. The result was the different schools of Gnosticism, and other forms of error and heresy, by which Christianity was subjected to greater peril than from persecution, or even from the false and antagonistic religions that confronted it.

How did Christianity overcome these oppositions, these

corrupting influences? By its compact organization, its unity under the Episcopate, its intense zeal and earnestness subordinated to discipline, and working in thorough harmony and co-operation.

We find through all the early conflicts of Christianity a complete, effective organization of all its forces in a kingdom, the Church of the living God. When the Church comes into view immediately after the Apostolic age, we find it as described by numerous authentic authors of those times, the same in all places, however widely separated, and it had extended itself throughout the civilized world. In every considerable city of every province of the widely extended Roman Empire, which embraced almost the whole world as then known, there was the Bishop with his Presbyters and Deacons, with his Deaconesses, readers and other orders of the laity, and all the brethren, each and all in their appointed places, working under direction and so in harmony, with the intensest zeal rightly directed, with a unity which gave irresistible strength and efficiency. Christianity was thoroughly organized. It was embodied in the Kingdom, the Church of Christ. All were baptized into the profession of the one Faith, the universal Creed of the Apostles, the watchword of Christians throughout the world. The same sacraments, rites and worship held all in loyal devotion to Christ. Corruption of doctrines and of life were repressed with promptness. The unworthy could find no place. Discipline was maintained.   Persecution from without helped to maintain purity and to promote that zeal and earnestness of Christian life of which martyrdom was the frequent crown.

The unity of the Church was in the Episcopate.   There was no one Bishop invested with supremacy.   Bishops, in all the essentials of their office, were everywhere equal. The Episcopate was one and undivided, and all the parts were held in perfect oneness, under the leadership and government of the Bishops, each with the advice and co-operation of his Crown of Presbyters.

The object was not self-enjoyment nor aggrandizement, but conquest and victory over sin, Satan and the world ; the conversion of souls, and the incorporation of those converted into the Body.   The missionary idea controlled the Church's development.   To extend the Kingdom was the purpose that guided all.   And thus it was that, after two centuries and more of persecution, the Christian Cross supplanted the Roman Eagle and the Church gave laws to the world.

Now, was this true and pure Christianity ?   That Christianity *was* such as we have described it, during the two centuries that followed the Apostolic age, we suppose no one will question.   It was, in fact, a kingdom that was not divided against itself.   And hence, instead of yielding to the powers that were arrayed against it, and which, had it not been what it was, would have destroyed it, it practically overcame all opposition.   Heathenism vanished before it. It carried the forces of social regeneration. It put an end to the demoralizing forms of wickedness. It was strong enough to make itself felt everywhere. It was a tremendous power for all that was good. It was able to compel recognition of its claims, as the Kingdom of Christ and of the Truth.

Now, was it part of Christ's plan that it should be so organized? Was it true that He did *not* intend to found a visible, spiritual kingdom, such as His Church was confessedly after His Apostles left it, and during the period of its sufferings and its greatest triumphs? Had it developed and taken on a form, such as was no part of the divine Idea? Strange as it may appear, there are some who so hold and teach. Indeed, such a view must of necessity be held by those who deny Episcopacy to be the Apostolic form of Church organization. For, if the Apostles, as instructed by Christ Himself, and guided in their action as in their teaching by His Spirit, left the Church organized imperfectly, or in some other manner, or left it to organize itself variously, or in whatever way might seem at any time expedient, and it did become from early in the second century onwards, as all admit that it did, a strong, consolidated kingdom with a gradation of orders, offices and active functions for all its members under Episcopal oversight and supervision, then, clearly, the design of Christ had been frustrated, and His religion almost at its beginning had been perverted.

But let us see what is His own teaching concerning the
manner and the means by which He would provide that
His truth should be conserved, perpetuated and made vic-
torious.   There is the strongest presumption that He who
had encountered Satan in the wilderness, and understood
His enemy, would so organize His system that it should
have the necessary strength to overcome Satan and his
hosts, and to carry out its full purposes of blessing for all
mankind.   And we find, that no sooner did He begin to
teach than He took up the message of the Baptist, "The
Kingdom of Heaven is at hand."   He proclaims His Gospel as "the Gospel of the Kingdom."   Very much of His
teaching was concerning this kingdom, and what it was to
be like.   His parables are, generally, parables of the Kingdom.   He taught how we were to enter it, and how we
were to grow into its spirit and life, and how it should
grow from small beginnings to greatness, majesty and beneficence.   He appointed its chief officers, prescribed the
powers they were to exercise, and promised to them officially, His perpetual presence.   He identified His Kingdom,
as it should exist in this world, with His Church visible,
and declared that the gates of Hell should not prevail
against it.   The last words He spoke to His Apostles,
before He ascended into Heaven, must have been solemn
words, of peculiar significancy, and they must have been
treasured as a priceless legacy.   They were the confirmation to the Apostles of the powers He had given them,

which they were to exercise by the Holy Ghost, they and their successors, in all times, and unto the uttermost parts of the earth.

The Apostles, when they were duly empowered for their work by the Holy Spirit, began their labors, in the sublime confidence of men who held a divine commission, and full authority and complete instructions for their guidance. As when the Tabernacle was to be built by Moses, the dwelling place of Jehovah, the place of meeting between God and His people, the design of which was afterwards to be more fully carried out in the Temple on Mount Zion, the antetype of the Christian Church, the construction proceeded in precise accordance with the pattern shown before in the Mount, so the Apostles builded, on a plan expressly given them by their Risen Lord, when for forty days He remained with them and "spake of the things pertaining to the Kingdom of God." This accounts for the manner in which they went forward in their work. They baptized all believers with their children, adding to the Church daily such as should be saved. They bound them to the profession of their doctrine, the Creed which they taught, long before they wrote the Gospels or the Epistles. They required all to abide in unity in what was called the Apostles' fellowship. They ensured this by frequent celebrations of the Holy Communion, called the Breaking of Bread, and the unvarying principles of a common ritual, the public prayers, the liturgy.

All the Apostles remained for some years in Jerusalem until this Mother Church was fully constituted, with James as its Bishop, with its Presbyters and Deacons, and its lay workers, its beneficence to the poor, its entire devotion to Christ and His cause, the model Church for the whole world. The Apostolic College was enlarged by S. Paul's admission into the number, and his fellow-helpers, Barnabas, Andronicus, Timothy and Titus, and many others. And wherever the Church was planted, it was unquestionably the same Church with its Apostle-Bishops, Elders and Deacons, its doctrines, sacraments, ritual and discipline. There was nothing tentative in their methods of organization. They made no mistakes to be afterwards corrected. Proceeding upon a plan which the Lord had given them, and guided by the Holy Spirit in its execution, the Church was the same as planted among Jewish and Gentile Christians, by Apostles to the Jews and to the Gentiles. It is very strange that all do not see the necessary inference to be drawn from what all writers of highest competency and authority admit, that James, the Lord's brother, was Bishop of Jerusalem, and that the Church took Episcopal form under the eyes of the Apostles. Were these Christ's Apostles? Were they inspired? Was, then, the Church, whose earliest development these divinely guided men were guiding, but a human scheme, of such orders of Ministry and such form of polity, as chance circumstances, or the caprice or judgment of men in any place might give it?

Not such was it, as a matter of fact. As modeled by the Apostles, it was a strong Episcopal organization. It was, as adapted to be in its constitution, powerfully aggressive everywhere. Clergy and laity, with perfect loyalty and devotion, worked together for the salvation of souls, for the spread of the Gospel under Apostolic leadership and oversight. The combined efforts of all in whatever was to be done, as decided by those in chief authority, made the Kingdom of Christ resistless in its strength. And so the Word of God grew mightily and prevailed. And no wonder. So it would now, if we could get rid of our congregationalism, if we would realize that we are an host marching and fighting under orders, and work together with the loyalty, earnestness and zeal of the Apostolic age.

You can now see clearly enough why it was that the Church of the second and third centuries was what we found it to be, and everybody knows it to have been. Unity does not grow out of heterogeneity. Varient and discordant forms of government do not easily coalesce. The Church was founded as *One*, and was so constituted that it should be a kingdom, with its regularly appointed officers, rulers, constitution, principles and fundamental laws—a kingdom not divided against itself.

If Jesus Christ did found in the world a kingdom, if His Church was that kingdom, and if, as He declared, it was to be perpetuated in all the essential elements which made it what it was, until it should be, in fact, universal, and the design of the Gospel should be realized in the proclamation of the Gospel everywhere, and to all mankind, then it follows that that same Institution is in the world to-day.   It is not difficult to trace it down through history, for its records are by no means obscure.   I need but refer to the Greek, Oriental and Russian branches, nor to the Latin or Roman.   Christianity was planted in Britain in the Apostolic, or immediately subsequent age.   The Church of England has its independent succession not derived from the Roman See.   The Roman usurpation maintained itself for a time over Church and State alike, but always against protest.   The protest became effectual in the sixteenth century, and the foreign influence was terminated, while the Church, as the State, preserved its identity unbroken, its intregrity unimpaired.   The Church was the same through all in its Ministry of Bishops, Priests and Deacons, its Scriptures, Creeds and Sacraments, its laws and ritual in all essential features.   Nothing that was primitive was destroyed.   All that was primitive was restored and preserved.   There was no essential change in polity, doctrine, worship or discipline.   This identity and unbroken succession and continuity is acknowledged by well informed students and writers of the Greeks, the old Catholics and even Romanists, like Courayer and Lingard, who have given dispassionate examination to the subject. In fact, no Church, Greek, Roman, or Protestant, has ever formally denied the validity of our Orders as preserved through and since the Reformation.

We, brethren, are a branch of this Apostolic Church, planted here in colonial times, organized fully with the Episcopate, after the Revolution, when we became a nation, with a strong foothold in every important center of influence in all the states and territories, ready everywhere for aggressive warfare against the hosts of sin and Satan, pledged to the accomplishment of the same work for which the Saviour called, and sent, and empowered His Apostles. Never was a branch of the Apostolic Church in a better position to do the Apostolic and catholic work for which the Church was founded.

With a brief statement of some of the requisites for doing that work, we may appropriately conclude this discourse.

First, it is obvious that we must *believe in* the Church as divine. So our Creed compels us. Man did not make it. It is made for him. It is founded by and upon Jesus Christ. It was all first in Him, as sent by the Father. He conferred of His powers upon His Apostles. By them the powers of the Ministry were distributed in the three Orders. But Christ Himself is the King. His Ministers are His ambassadors. He retains to Himself His intransmissible Headship as the Shepherd and Bishop of souls. Our first duty is loyalty to Him. Loyalty involves the most unwavering faith and undivided fealty. We must do whatever He commands us.   We must receive those whom He sends to us and obey them as those who are appointed to watch for our souls.   The Word, the Faith, the Sacraments, the Worship, are ours from Christ to receive, to use, to profit by, to extend.   Everything essential in the Church, everything given it by the first Apostles of Christ, taught of Him personally and by the Holy Ghost, must be believed and acted on by us as a vital part of Christian faith and duty.

The Church being divine, and for the great end of preserving and extending the Faith whereby we are saved, it follows that we must believe in this instrumentality. The Gospel is to be made known by the Church.   We ought to have, if we expect success, the most undoubting confidence in the Church as the agency of Christ Himself, His own institution for the conversion, the moral elevation, the sanctification and salvation of men.   Let the Church call forth all her latent forces.   Let her use her functions. Let her put forth her divinely given powers.   Let her wield aright the sword of the Spirit which is in her hands, and we shall see such results as were witnessed in the early ages.   Christ is in her of a truth.   Believe this, and let your works accompany and prove your faith.

It is necessary also, for such success as we are taught to pray for, when we rightly say "Thy Kingdom come," that we do what we can that Christ's Kingdom may stand in its integrity.   On the one hand, the officers must fulfil the work for which they are responsible; and on the other, the brethren, all, men and women, must sustain them, work for and with them, as faithful soldiers under command, not dictating their policy, not complaining and finding fault, and giving themselves to detraction, not destroying unity of effect, which depends upon a headship, not dividing the kingdom against itself, but co-operating, helping to save souls and edify the Body, and thus working out their own salvation. If, when Timothy was sent to Ephesus and Titus to Crete, to set in order the things that were wanting, to ordain Elders and Deacons, and to administer discipline, and whatever else belonged to the Episcopal office, their people had replied, as they would have done had they been Independents or Congregationalists, *we* can ordain our own Elders, *we* can set things in order, *we* want none of your interference, the Gospel would have had but poor success in these populous communities. Not guided by a head, their action would have been narrow, selfish, individualistic, obstructive. There would have been no unity. The kingdom divided against itself would have been brought to desolation. And so also a like result of failure would have followed all sinful indulgencies, conformity to the world in its excesses and its vices, all lack of earnestness in working, liberality in giving, holiness in life, on the part of the members of the Church of Christ.

Finally, my brethren, remember that in your baptism,

when you were entered into Christ's Kingdom, you were sworn to fight manfully against the world, the flesh, and the Devil, and to continue Christ's faithful soldiers and servants unto your lives' end.   Glorious will be your reward if you fulfil this your oath of allegiance and of loyalty.   Your King and Lord needs this service from you. The Church needs it.   When all the hosts of Satan are arrayed in deadly hostility against Christ and His Church, and the world and sin are his powerful allies, and every power and every subtlety are used to thwart our King and to overturn, or divide, or prevent the progress of His Kingdom, it is a shame that any should be seen fighting in Satan's ranks, with the sign of the Cross not obliterated from their foreheads !   In whose ranks are you marching?   Are you with Christ?   Do you belong in heart and life to His embattled hosts, fighting manfully against His enemies?   Or are you only professedly with Him, really against Him?   God grant to us all fidelity in the station appointed for us.